THE
POWER
OF
WE

How to Influence and Build Stronger Brands, Communities, and Movements Through Unity

PRASHANTH GODREHAL

Dedication

To My Parents
For Always Believing in Me

Table of Contents

Table of Contents

Preface

The Power of We

It's Saturday during the month of August, the year 2020. I'm sitting in my home office on an old, worn couch. It's the peak of COVID-19 pandemic, the fourth month of remote work, and the clock reads 11:00 PM. I'm drafting a question for a new online community I joined recently when a wave of annoyance hit me. My 3-year-old son had been asking me all evening to take him to the park, but I kept postponing, losing track of time as I immersed myself in the online world.

As I sit there reflecting, I begin noticing a pattern. I am now part of 10 online communities—coaching, marketing, writing, music, cycling, spirituality, and more—all hosted-on platforms like WhatsApp and Facebook. These communities are becoming an integral part of my life, and I'm spending more and more time engaging with them.

It's not just me. My wife, Renuka, has formed her own set of communities around yoga, cooking, and music apps like Star Maker. Meanwhile, my daughter, Kshama, has immersed herself in groups centred on K-pop, online brands, and music.

These digital spaces are shaping our lives in ways I hadn't anticipated. They're creating a sense of collective identity - a "We-ness" - around shared interests and causes. They influence what we buy, what we explore, and how we make decisions. We don't need much interaction with the outside world anymore; we just ask the community for answers. Some groups are more influential than others, but they all contribute to a growing sense of belonging. That night, a realization hit me. I've always prided myself on having my views and interests. Yet here I am, subtly influenced by the groups I've joined, performing actions I might have rejected outright just a few months earlier.

I became both curious and worried. Is this a new phenomenon, or has it always existed in some form? As I dig deeper, I come across Dr. Robert Cialdini's ground-breaking work in the latest edition of *Influence: The Psychology of Persuasion*. In this 2015 edition, Cialdini introduces a new principle—"Unity." It feels like an epiphany. I've been a fan of Dr. Cialdini's work since 2005, but the Unity principle perfectly encapsulates what I was experiencing. The idea that shared identity and belonging can be such powerful drivers of influence resonates deeply.

My curiosity takes me further into fields like social psychology, neuroscience, and history. With the Unity principle as a lens, I start seeing patterns everywhere - on battlefields, in businesses, and in sports teams. Time and again, unity has been the edge that small, focused groups have used to defeat larger, more divided entities.

In the digital age, the power of Unity is even more compelling. Online communities magnify this force, creating tight-knit groups with shared values and goals. It's a phenomenon that demands attention. The deeper I go, the clearer the puzzle becomes. Unity is the psychological glue that binds groups together, making them stronger and more cohesive. It's not just about fostering connection—it's about shaping beliefs and driving behaviours in profound ways.

This realization sparks a research project of my own. I start exploring how businesses, social movements, revolutions, and sports teams leverage the power of Unity. My obsession grows as I hunt for patterns and commonalities. I ask myself: Are businesses already harnessing this power, even if unconsciously? Could these principles be systematically applied to grow ventures, inspire social causes, and create a lasting impact?

Piece by piece, I uncover a universal truth. Politics, business, culture, and religion—all these realms share a common thread: the power of Unity. A strong sense of "We-ness" can launch a brand, spark a movement, or even fuel a revolution. At the same time, it can be weaponized for darker purposes, as seen in criminal organizations, terrorist networks, and manipulative regimes.

This journey leads me to identify the essential elements of collective identity—elements that enable brands and businesses to grow rapidly, resonate emotionally, and create a lasting impact. This book is the culmination of that exploration. Together, we'll examine how Unity has shaped history, how it operates in today's world, and how you can harness it to achieve extraordinary results. Whether you are launching a business, leading a team, or building a community, the power of Unity can accelerate your growth and amplify your impact.

Even if you are not creating something, understanding this psychological principle gives you a clearer perspective on the forces shaping businesses, politics, religions, and our everyday lives. The secrets are all around us; we just need to unlock them.

Let's begin.

How is this Book organized?

I organized the book for easy reading so you can complete it in just a few hours. At the same time, it is structured as a workbook so you can take your time, reading chapter by chapter, to gain a deeper understanding and apply its findings to your work and communities.

The book is divided into three parts:

- **Part 1: Understanding the Power of Unity**
  In this part, I explain what makes unity such a powerful force in human realms, diving into the psychology and evolutionary forces that drive it.

- **Part 2: The Core Blueprint**
  I introduce the core blueprint for aspiring leaders and entrepreneurs, showing how strong communities, and brands are built using the power of "We-ness." This section includes actionable steps and examples from diverse fields, balancing business insights with historical and financial perspectives. It provides

essential elements to understand how "We-ness" forms and sustains itself.

- **Part 3: Observing We-ness in Action**
  I explore how "We-ness" manifests in various settings, especially on digital and social media platforms, while examining the darker side of unity. I conclude the chapter by discussing Unity with diversity thrives and Unity is not about uniformity, with exploring a Hindu way of living and some ideas of how the unity in future looks. I conclude by showing how we can harness the power of unity in our lives and work.

Thank you for your interest in this book! I hope it excites you as much as it does me to explore and understand the force of unity.

PART I

WHAT MAKES UNITY POWERFUL FOR INFLUENCE

Chapter 1:

The Age of "We"

Take a moment to consider the world around you. Over the last 3 decades since the internet spread and over the last one and a half decades, when social media has taken over, we're more connected than at any point in human history. Today, social media platforms connect billions of people across the globe in real-time.

At times, movements can spark from a single tweet or Instagram post and ripple to create global change. Brands are no longer just selling products; they create communities fostering tribes. Sports clubs, movie stars, musicians, artists, and politicians are building their communities of followers or supporters.

We are living in a world that often celebrates the individual, personal freedom, and self-identification. But now we're witnessing a powerful shift towards collective identity, or "We-ness."

So, whether you are part of a fitness team, a social movement, or a dedicated fanbase, chances are you've felt the pull of "We-ness" - that magnetic force that draws people together, creating something far greater than the sum of its parts.

The Power of Collective Identity

What is it about "We-ness" that's so compelling? Why do people flock to it, and how does it wield such influence? At its core, "We-ness" taps into a fundamental human need: the desire to belong. Psychologists have long understood that humans are inherently social creatures. We seek out connection and community because they provide safety, support, and a sense of identity. But "We-ness" goes beyond just belonging; it's about merging individual identity with that of a group, creating a powerful collective identity that can drive behaviour, shape decisions, and inspire action.

The thing most likely to guide a person's behavioural decision is the most potent or instructive yes aspect of the whole situation; instead, it is the one that is most prominent in the consciousness at the time of decision.

Consider the phenomenon of fandoms in pop culture. Take sports fan clubs like the IPL clubs in India or international football clubs like Real Madrid and Manchester United. The Fans don't just enjoy the games; they identify as part of a collective community. Many fans attend conventions dressed as their favourite characters, engage in online discussions, and support the franchise with unwavering loyalty.

It isn't just about sports or entertainment; it's about belonging to something bigger than oneself. The sports fanbase, comic movies, or online game fandom are a perfect example of "We-ness" in action. This shared identity unites millions of different backgrounds, cultures, and geographies.

From Individualism to "We-ness"

The last many decades, especially in the western world, championed individualism, and have successfully influenced most societies throughout recent history. The French Revolution championed the idea of freedom and liberty, embedding personal success, self-reliance, and individual achievement as ultimate goals in the cultural narrative.

"Be yourself," "Stand out from the crowd," and "Make your mark" are mantras that have guided generations of motivational talks. And while there's nothing inherently wrong with individualism, it's becoming clear that in today's interconnected world, focusing solely on oneself can be limiting.

The rise of "We-ness" challenges this notion by emphasizing the power of the collective. It's not about diminishing the individual but recognizing that actual influence often comes from being part of something larger. Whether in business, social movements, sports, religion, or even entertainment, those who understand and harness the power of collective identity are often the most successful. We will see how this works in various areas later. Consider the last significant social or political movement that captured your attention for now.

Perhaps if you are in your 40s like me, it is the Ram Janmabhoomi movement that led to the rise of the BJP, or the Brexit movement that called Britain to move out of the European Union, the Cauvery Calling movement by Sadhguru bringing together people from all over India for saving river Cauvery, or the fitness movement especially of marathon's in various cities, "Save Palestine" movement and many you can recollect.

In any of these movements, the important aspect is to look at what made these movements so powerful. It isn't just the message; Instead, it is the sense of Unity and shared purpose among the community that rallied millions worldwide. These movements didn't just speak to individuals; instead, they created a collective identity—a "We" that is impossible to ignore. This conveys the idea that you are not alone. You belong to something bigger. That together we succeed and divide, we fail. That united, we are capable of more.

Why "We" Matters Now?

First, let's discuss why this "We" matters more now than ever. It is not "We-ness" that is a new phenomenon or didn't exist. "We-ness" is a core part of human evolution, and it is deeply rooted in our nature and is part of tribal culture that we shall discuss in Chapter 3.

However, as we have entered into an era of the internet with information overload, there is a significant shift, and it is due to the pervasiveness of social media and other online platforms that have transformed how we communicate, share ideas and form communities.

Geography once limited us, but now we instantly connect with like-minded individuals across the globe. These digital spaces breed 'We-ness,' enabling us to form communities and movements that seemed impossible just a few decades ago. As our world becomes more interconnected, we increasingly realize how deeply our actions intertwine with those of others. "We-ness" offers a framework for understanding and addressing these challenges by emphasizing the importance of collective effort, shared responsibility, and the dangers of this change.

We-ness isn't just a trendy buzzword or a fleeting concept; it's a profound force shaping how we connect, lead, and ultimately influence. The age of "We" has always existed, but now it's more relevant than ever.

Luckily, we have scientific evidence from social psychology today on how this Unity works and why it is powerful. It is also important to remember there is a dark side to Unity that many ignore! We shall discover how to use Unity as a powerful tool for good and be prepared to overcome harmful effects.

Chapter 2:

The Psychology of Influence:

From "I" to "We"

The significance which is in Unity is an eternal wonder."

Rabindranath Tagore

We often imagine charismatic individuals who can sway minds and shape decisions with words and actions when we think of influence. The focus is usually on the "I"—the person who stands out, commands attention, and drives change. However, in the context of "We-ness," influence takes on a different dimension. It's not just about the power of one, but the power of many.

Understanding the psychology behind this shift from "I" to "We" is crucial if we want to harness collective influence effectively.

The "We-ness" Effect: How It Shapes Influence

So, what does this mean for an individual, parent, business, or community in terms of influence? How does "We-ness" impact how we influence others, how can we harness it, and how do we get influenced by others? The answer lies in understanding that influence is most effective when it's not about imposing one's will on others, but about aligning with a group's identity and values.

When people feel part of a "We," they're more likely to be receptive to ideas, more willing to take action, and more committed to a cause. This is because "We-ness" fosters a sense of ownership and responsibility. When you are part of a collective identity, the success or failure of the group feels personal—it's not just about "them," it's about "us." This collective identity or ego creates a much bigger force.

The Roots of Social Identity

To grasp the full power of "We-ness," we must start with a fundamental concept in social psychology: social identity. Social identity theory, first developed by Henri Tajfel and John Turner in the 1970s, explains how individuals categorize themselves and others into groups and how these group identities influence behaviour.

According to this theory, our social identities—based on nationality, religion, profession, or fandom—significantly shape our self-concept. Think about the various groups you belong to. You might identify as a parent, a professional, a fan of a particular sports team, or a member of a specific community, belong to a particular state, have a linguistic identity like a Kannada/Telugu speaking community, religion, or at a significant level of belonging state, nation and even continent. Each identity influences how you see yourself and interact with the world.

When you are at a sports game, for instance, you don't just see yourself as an individual; you see yourself as part of a larger group—the fans, the "we" that cheers for the same team, wear the same colours, and shares the same hopes and frustrations. Identifying with a group is more than just a cognitive exercise; it's deeply emotional.

When we adopt a group identity, we also adopt the emotions, values, and behaviours associated with that group.

This is why group identities can be so powerful—they shape not just what we think, but how we feel and act.

From Self-Identity to Social Identity

The shift from "I" to "We" happens when our social identity becomes more salient than our identity. This doesn't mean we lose our sense of self; in certain contexts, our group identity becomes the primary lens through which we see the world. Consider the phenomenon of "basking in reflected glory" (BIRGing), a concept in social psychology that describes how people derive pride and self-esteem from the successes of their groups.

When your favourite sports team wins, you are likely to feel a sense of personal pride, even if you had nothing to do with the victory. You might say, "We won!" even though you were just watching from the stands or on TV. This is because, at that moment, your social identity as a fan becomes more prominent than your identity. You see yourself as part of the "we," and the team's victory feels like your own.

Conversely, there's also "cutting off reflected failure" (CORFing), where individuals distance themselves from a group after a loss or failure to protect their self-esteem. After a disappointing loss, fans might say, "They lost," instead of

"We lost," to psychologically separate themselves from the failure. These examples illustrate how fluid the boundary between "I" and "We" can be. Our social identities are dynamic and context-dependent, and they can significantly influence our thoughts, feelings, and behaviours.

The Power of Group Norms

One of the key ways in which "We-ness" exerts influence is through group norms. Norms are the unwritten rules that govern behaviour within a group. They tell us what is acceptable, what is expected, and what is valued. When we identify with a group, we're more likely to conform to its norms because doing so reinforces our social identity and strengthens our bond with the group.

Consider how group norms operate in a professional setting. In a highly collaborative team, for example, there might be a strong norm of open communication and mutual support. New members quickly learn that speaking up, sharing ideas, and helping colleagues are expected behaviours. Those who adhere to these norms are seen as valuable team members, while those who don't may be marginalized or excluded.

The influence of group norms can be incredibly powerful, often overriding personal preferences or inclinations. Hence, "We-ness" can be such a potent force in shaping behaviour. When people see themselves as part of a group, they're motivated to align their actions with the group's expectations, even if it means going against their inclinations.

A striking example is the famous Asch conformity experiments conducted in the 1950s. Participants were asked to match the length of a line on one card with one of three lines on another. The task was simple, and the correct answer was obvious.

However, among the 6 participants who were placed in a group, 5 were confederates in the experiment. After a few tests, the confederates started deliberately choosing the wrong answer. The lone participant who was neutral started to conform to the group's choice, even though it was incorrect. This demonstrates how the desire to fit in with the group can lead people to conform, even when it contradicts their judgment.

Recent neuroscience studies reveal that resisting group conformity activates the same neural pathways as those triggered by acute physical pain. To avoid this discomfort, individuals often choose to conform to the group. Now that we have covered a bit of psychology, another equally crucial element exists.

And it is evolutionary forces that drive us towards Unity and how being united helped the homo sapiens survive and even thrive over the millennia. Let's understand these in the next chapter.

Chapter 3:

The Tribal Mindset: How Evolution Shapes "We-ness"

Even the weak become strong when they are united."

Friedrich Schiller

In the previous chapter, we talked about the powerful psychological force behind this "we-ness."

In this chapter, let's explore the evolutionary roots of the tribal mindset and how this deep-seated instinct influences our modern-day behaviour. We will draw on social studies and evolutionary research to understand how "We-ness" has shaped human history and discuss its implications for contemporary society.

The Evolutionary Origins of "We-ness"

To understand the power of "We-ness," we must first look at our evolutionary past. Pre-civilization humans lived in small, tightly knit groups where cooperation was essential for survival.

These groups, or tribes, provided protection, resources, and social bonds critical in a world filled with opposing tribes, predators, and environmental dangers. Evolutionary psychologists argue that the human brain evolved to prioritize group cohesion and social bonding because these traits increased our ancestors' chances of survival.

In his book *The Social Conquest of Earth*, biologist E.O. Wilson explains that human success as a species is primarily due to our ability to form and maintain complex social groups. These groups allowed early humans to hunt together, share food, defend against threats, and care for each other's offspring.

The benefits of group living led to the development of what is known as the "tribal mindset." This mindset is characterized by strong in-group loyalty, a tendency to favour members of one's group over outsiders, and a deep-seated need to belong. These traits were advantageous in ancestral environments because they promoted group cohesion and cooperation, which were critical for survival.

However, they also laid the groundwork for some of the challenges we face today, such as intergroup conflict and prejudice, which we discuss later. For now, one of the critical components of the tribal mindset is the ability to recognize and respond to group membership.

This is where the concept of "We-ness" comes into play. Our brains are wired to quickly identify who is "us" and who is "them" based on cues such as appearance, language, behaviour, shared beliefs, values, struggles, and even sufferings. This ability to categorize people into in-groups and out-groups is a fundamental aspect of human social cognition, and it underpins much of our social behaviour.

The Power of In-Group Favouritism

One of the most well-documented effects of the tribal mindset is in-group favouritism—the tendency to prefer and prioritize the well-being of those who belong to our group over those who do not. This behaviour has been observed in countless social studies and experiments, highlighting the deep-rooted nature of "We-ness" in human psychology.

In one classic study, the Robbers Cave Experiment, psychologist Muzafer Sherif demonstrated how easily in-group favouritism can be induced.

Sherif and his colleagues took a group of boys to a summer camp and randomly divided them into two groups. Throughout the experiment, the boys quickly developed strong group identities, naming their groups the "Eagles" and the "Rattlers." As competition between the groups was introduced, the boys began to display intense loyalty to their group and hostility towards the other. This experiment showed how quickly and powerfully "We-ness" can be created, leading to strong in-group favouritism and out-group antagonism.

In-group favouritism isn't just a quirk of human behaviour; it has significant evolutionary advantages. By favouring those who belong to our group, we increase the chances of mutual support, cooperation, and resource sharing—behaviours that would have been essential for survival in ancestral environments.

The Role of Social Studies in Understanding Tribalism

Social studies have provided valuable insights into how "We-ness" operates in the context of tribalism. One important concept is "social identity theory," developed by psychologists Henri Tajfel and John Turner. According to this theory, people derive a significant part of their self-esteem from group memberships. As a result, they are motivated to enhance the status of their in-group (the group to which they belong) and, by extension, themselves. This often leads to in-group favouritism and out-group discrimination.

Tajfel's experiments demonstrated how easily group identities can be created and how quickly they can lead to biased behaviour. In one study, participants were randomly assigned to different groups based on arbitrary criteria, such as their preference for certain paintings.

Despite the lack of fundamental differences between the groups, participants quickly began favouring their group members over others, even when it meant sacrificing potential rewards. It showed that even minimal group identities could trigger strong feelings of "We-ness" and lead to discriminatory behaviour. Another key finding from social studies is the "contact hypothesis," which suggests that increasing contact between members of different groups can reduce prejudice and improve intergroup relations.

This idea was famously tested during the desegregation of schools in the United States, where it was found that when children of different racial backgrounds were brought together in cooperative settings, their prejudices often diminished. This research highlights the potential for overcoming the darker aspects of "We-ness" by fostering positive interactions between groups.

The Dark Side of "We-ness": Tribalism and Conflict

While "We-ness" has many benefits, it also has a dark side. The same instincts that promote group cohesion and cooperation can also lead to tribalism, where loyalty to one's group becomes so strong that it fosters division, conflict, and even violence. This darker aspect of the tribal mindset has been a source of tension and strife throughout human history.

Evolutionary research suggests that intergroup conflict is a natural extension of the tribal mindset. Competition for resources such as food, territory, and mates in ancestral environments often led to conflict between groups. Those most loyal to their group and most hostile to outsiders were more likely to survive and pass on their genes.

As a result, humans evolved a propensity for intergroup conflict, which continues to manifest in various forms today, from ethnic and religious conflicts to political polarization.

In today's world, the conflict for resources if not as severe as our ancestors experienced, newer conflicts have risen due to different ideologies, such as religious, political, and moral ones, that can be related to "We-ness." As Dr. Cialdini mentions in his book ***Influence, Psychology of Persuasion,*** Unity is defined by the characteristics of these categories that the "We" group members tend to feel "at one" with and merge with one another. They are the categories in which the conduct of one member influences the self-esteem of other members; put simply, the "we" is the shared me.

Three constraints have emerged:

1. First, members of "We" based groups favour the outcomes and welfare of fellow members over those of non-members by a mile. For example, members of rival work groups that each included two humans and two robots not only held more positive attitudes towards their teammates but also went so far as to hold more positive attitudes towards their team robots than towards the rival team robots and humans

2. Second, we group members are highly likely to use the preferences and actions of fellow members to guide their own, which is the tendency that ensures group solidarity.

3. Finally, these parties are just to favour and follow, and they have risen evolutionarily as ways to advantage our "we" groups and, ultimately, ourselves.

PART II

THE BLUEPRINT OF FORMING WE-GROUP

Chapter 4:

Building the "We": Foundations of Collective Identity

In the vast mosaic of human experience, the most compelling and enduring stories are those of unity. Whether it's a nation, kingdom, sports team, a grassroots movement, or a global brand, the ability to forge a collective identity—what we've been calling "We-ness"—is a cornerstone of influence. But how exactly is this sense of "We" constructed? What foundational elements transform a collection of individuals into a cohesive group with a shared identity? In this chapter, we'll explore the building blocks of collective identity. We'll examine how shared values, goals, rituals, and symbols create powerful "We-ness" and how you can apply these principles to build strong, influential communities.

The Blueprint of "We-ness"

The blueprint of "We-ness" includes many elements, but predominantly, it can be identified as one that is to form a group and to sustain and have a strong "We-ness," there are nine core elements.

These are,

1. Who is In / Who is Out?
2. Collective Values
3. Beliefs
4. Collective Vision
5. Common Enemy
6. Leadership
7. Shared Language
8. Everyday Rituals, Symbols & Anchors
9. Stories and Narratives

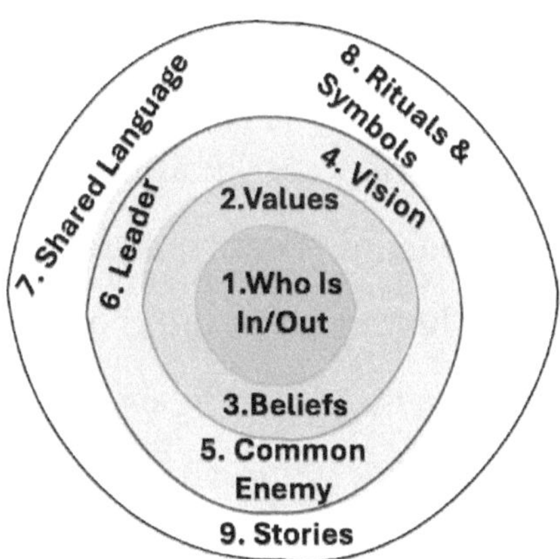

Figure 1: 9 elements of unity

Over the following chapters, I shall explore each of these elements and the role they play in-depth and, more importantly, how they apply to different areas of society, such as business, social movements, and religions. I attempt to show you how these elements are common when it comes be it forming, sustaining and growing the we-groups be it political, business, or any other social groups that we all encounter every day.

The Blueprint of "We-ness": Who is in/Who is out?

The first and most important of "We-ness" is defining who is in and who is out! With better clarity of who is in the group and who is outside, the influence becomes much faster and safer, creating the groups to flourish. In business parlance, this becomes who our "audience" is! Everything starts from here.

One of Steve Jobs' most famous statements emphasizing the importance of knowing the audience Apple must serve comes from his internal meeting with the Apple team in 1997 after his return to the company. Jobs clearly defined Apple's focus on a specific audience, which helped crystallize the company's vision and strategy. Here's a key excerpt: "One of the things I've always found is that you've got to start with the customer experience and work backwards to the technology. You can't start with the technology and try to figure out where you will try to sell it.

As we have tried to develop a strategy and a vision for Apple, it started with: What incredible benefits can we give the customer? Where can we take the customer? Not starting with, 'Let's sit down with the engineers and figure out what awesome technology we have and then how we're going to market that.'" This statement illustrates how Jobs believed in first understanding exactly *who* Apple was serving—who was "in" their audience and, by implication, who was "out."

He emphasized the importance of knowing the customer intimately, defining the focus of Apple's innovation and ensuring the company delivers meaningful products. This concept underlines that defining "Who is In / Who is Out" is crucial for any collective identity or brand-building strategy. Knowing who you are serving can create products, stories, and experiences that resonate deeply, fostering a strong sense of unity and belonging around your brand.

For any unity to thrive, everyone in this group will become an advocate, a participant, a consumer, a listener, a viewer or co-creator, a deeply committed member, and potentially even a leader who helps grow this group beyond.

Because in any group, one cannot effectively serve, speak to, or rally someone if they don't understand (a) who they are, (b) what they care about, (c) what's wrong, (d) what fear's, and (e) where they'd love to go.

Like you are in his head, you already know what he needs. It also does one other thing: it helps ensure you are truly connected to your tribe and group and care about them.

Very often, because they are you when you are in that tribe, everyone will feel the authenticity, and the ability to truly connect and serve goes up exponentially.

For any business brand to build, it starts with knowing exactly

1. What is the bigger problem that needs to be solved?

2. Where do they live?

3. What's their mindset?

4. What do they think about?

5. What is he/her life like?

6. What are the needs or aspirations, hopes, and desires?

For example, take the example of Nike; it sells a lifestyle and mindset that aligns with the values of determination, perseverance, and excellence. It's a rallying cry that unites athletes and aspiring athletes worldwide. It creates a sense of "We-ness" by appealing to the shared identity of those who strive for greatness, regardless of their circumstances.

Again, the "We-ness" also excludes the group. It makes a case where the people are not part of their group. Apple caters to groups that value design and innovation vs. those who value cost and cheapness. For a company catering to healthy food, it is clear that its audience is those interested in health and fitness, and out are those who prefer junk foods.

An interesting case study is of Baba Ramdev, the founder of Patanjali. Baba Ramdev, who started by teaching Yoga and Pranayama and later decided to promote healthy living, "I'm going to start a company focused on Ayurvedic and natural products to take on MNCs and Allopathic drugs".

Rather than just come up with one company that does Ayurveda or herbal-related products such as Himalaya, Dabur, and Patanjali, it was clear who they are against and what their audience is. Baba Ramdev has a great following, and this stand allowed him to create a much stronger community and culture to bind his followers and also opened vast numbers of followers to the Ayurveda and non-allopathic treatments that had been turned off for years.

Chapter 5:

The Collective Values & Beliefs

The great lesson is that unity is behind all. Call it God, Love, or Spirit. Allah, Jehovah—it is the same unity that animates all life."

- Swami Vivekananda

Having a set audience who are "In" is the first step, but the glue that bonds them is to be of emotional and psychological and this happens through the values and beliefs that become part of the group. At the heart of every successful collective identity lies shared values or principles.

The values become the guiding principles and aspirations that give a group its purpose and direction. Without core values, "We-ness" lacks substance; it becomes a hollow concept rather than a driving force. Be it spiritual, social, sports, or business groups need to have a set of core values (guiding principles) and beliefs to keep the members together.

The importance of setting values

In the business world, brands that cultivate strong collective identities align their values with those of their customers. Take the case of Amazon, it is the most powerful internet company. Jeff Bezos, the founder was very clear from the beginning about how he wanted the company to be formed and to be known. He ensured that he clearly defined the core values that are guiding principles. It says Amazon wants to be Earth's most customer-centric company.

Amazon lists four core values (or "guiding principles") that are:

- Customer obsession rather than competitor focus
- Passion for invention
- Commitment to operational excellence
- Long-term thinking

Another example, I have personally found very appealing is the company Patagonia, the outdoor clothing company. Patagonia's commitment to environmental sustainability isn't just a corporate value; it's a shared value that resonates deeply with its customers, employees and everyone associated including partners. This kind of shared alignment creates a firm "We-ness" between the brand and its community, fostering loyalty and advocacy.

Values in social and political system

To understand more about values, we can also think about some of the we-groups from history. For example, in the context of the Indian freedom movement, there existed many different we-groups. Though they shared the same purpose—freedom from the British—their values and vision differed in how they wanted to achieve their goal and their group behaviour. For example, the Gandhian movement shared values of non-violence, equality, and self-sufficiency. In contrast, the Netaji Indian National Movement had shared values of Self-governance, Use of Force if necessary, and Hard work. These values weren't just abstract concepts; they were the movement's lifeblood, shaping its goals and inspiring countless individuals to join the cause. =The collective identity that each movement created wasn't just about being a part of a group; it was about being part of a group with a clear, powerful mission that united its followers.

Common Beliefs

Having values and guiding principles is excellent, but how do you make the group follow them without being reminded externally? It calls for instilling strong beliefs. Building on the collective identity depends on shared beliefs. These are beliefs that bind the group together, where they stand up and say,

"This is what I believe. This is what my heart says is true. I will bring this core set of values to this group, this venture, this endeavour, this movement." Having this set of beliefs brings clarity, strength, and specificity. The values that are pretty well shared in the tribe/we-group ultimately become statements of strong beliefs. Again, the beliefs that one group harbours seem blind beliefs to another group, but when it comes to collective identity, beliefs play a significant role.

Many companies have written forms of code of conduct or a set of beliefs they must adhere to. So, having a single sentence, like "all beings are created equal, regardless of race, sex, ability, or anything else." "We design the best products in the world." It is clear, specific, and easy for anyone to "get."

Same time, it is nice to build beautifully expressing beliefs with absolute clarity, but if group members do not instantly get it, then that expression is inadequate. So, making beliefs become a day-to-day part of expression, making it an automatic process, is essential.

From a messaging standpoint, this constant reminder gives a strong statement for people to say "yes" or "no" to. The group wants people to say one or the other. Strong ideas, businesses, ventures, and movements all provoke strong reactions. That's a good thing. If people don't feel strongly, they won't act strongly. Nor will they share or become members of your community. From a team-building standpoint, the beliefs also serve a crucial role later in the process, when any group assembles a team to help you grow your venture. It becomes a vital decision-making tool to see who's in and out, and whether it's OK for people to be out. It's OK for people not to belong and not actually to have that same set of shared beliefs.

Jeff Bezos was known for consistently communicating Amazon's four core principles since the day the company launched in 1995 in many of his meetings and public appearances. To build a successful company it must have a strong corporate culture and to build that Bezos communicated the values that make up that culture every day.

For example, the first core value of Amazon is *"Customer obsession rather than competitor focus". Jeff* Bezos reminded Amazonians often to pay attention to competitors, but to obsess over customers in many meetings. Zappos is another company that gives a powerful example of a mission-driven brand built upon the Zappos Family Core Values, a deliberate set of openly expressed values and beliefs. Ostensibly a "shoe" company, Zappos is something much bigger. They are a billion-dollar venture built upon the dual quest to create the best culture in the world and the best customer service in the world. Everything revolves around the core values and beliefs.

In fact, in the first few years of the Zappos, new employees after an initial few months at the company, were offered thousands of dollars to leave. It is a test. If you truly buy into the core beliefs and mission of the company, you'll laugh at the money. But on the other hand, if you don't truly believe and just focus on money, you'll take it and run, which is better for everyone. Outside of business, we can see how the beliefs are essential in some of the strongest we groups we have in society, such as the military. Luckily, I had a short stint to experience this when I was 18 years old.

Beliefs are the core part of the elite army.

It's 1992, and I'm an 18-year-old brimming with excitement as I step off the train from Bangalore to Prayagraj (then Allahabad), where the military campus looms large with its aura of discipline and purpose. This is my chance to join the National Defence Academy (NDA) and fulfil my dream of being part of the defence forces.

I grew up far from any military influence—no one in my family or extended family had ever served. Yet something about the collective identity of the military fascinated me. The camaraderie, the shared mission, and the unwavering sense of belonging pulled me in. Despite the lack of role models, I developed a strong urge to join the defence forces and finally appeared for the NDA entrance exam. I cleared the written test and received a call for the interview and psychology assessment. When I arrive at the campus, the intensity of the environment grips me immediately. The air feels different— serious yet energizing. Over the next four days, I was immersed in the heart of military culture, and I began to see how deeply the Army's beliefs shape its people. Every officer, every candidate, and every interaction reinforce one truth: The Army stands for national security, integrity, and unwavering loyalty.

The military's values aren't just written on walls or recited in meetings—they're lived. The officers make it clear what is accepted and what isn't. They speak with conviction about what it means to be part of the Army. To join, you must align with their core values and beliefs. This isn't negotiable. As I sit with my fellow candidates, I can see it clearly: the military isn't just a career; it's a way of life. And this collective identity—this "We-ness"—is what makes them so strong. It's a filter, determining who belongs and who doesn't. And that's okay. Not everyone is meant to be part of this group, but for those who are, these shared beliefs become their anchor.

Looking back, this experience taught me the power of belief in building unity. The military's collective identity is more than a tool for decision-making—it's the glue that binds its people together, ensuring everyone is on the same page. It's a lesson that applies not just to national defence but to any group striving to create something meaningful together. Researchers have conducted the study of interest and employed a time-honoured military tactic to instil a sense of group cohesion. After assigning participants to teams, the researchers asked some teams to walk together in step for a time; they asked others to walk together for the same amount of time, but normally. Later, all team members played an economic game in which they could either maximize the chance of increasing their financial gain or forgo that opportunity to ensure the teammates would do well financially.

Members of teams that had marched together were 50% more cooperative towards their teammates than were those who had just walked together normally. A follow-up study helps explain why. Initial synchrony led to a feeling of unity, which led to a greater willingness to sacrifice personal gain for the group's greater good. It is no wonder that marching in unison is still employed in military training, even though the battlefield technique disappeared a long ago. It is worth it as a unity-building technique, as it accounts for its retention.

Again, the caution to note here is that the very beliefs that serve to bring people together and stand for their values can also be the cause for becoming too rigid. You can commonly see that in groups, few hold on to beliefs so firmly that they cannot reconcile with others. Making sure the beliefs do not become too rigid is essential for group survival.

Chapter 6:

The Collective Vision & Common Enemy

"Coming together is a beginning. Keeping together is progress. Working together is a success."

Henry Ford

The next element that becomes most important is the collective vision and goals of the "We-group" stands for. Unless the values and beliefs are not paired with a clear vision and actionable goals that give the group something to strive toward, the group doesn't stand. Vision and goals provide direction and a sense of purpose, turning values into tangible outcomes.

When people see that their efforts contribute to a larger, meaningful objective, their commitment to the group—and the collective identity—strengthens.

Consider the goals of a sports team. The concrete objectives that drive the team forward are winning games, securing championships, and breaking records. These goals aren't just about personal achievement and fulfilling the team's and its supporters' collective ambition.

The same principle applies to any group or organization. Whether the goal is to launch a new product, advocate for social change, or simply build a stronger community, it must be clear, compelling, and aligned with the group's shared values. The we-group, with values and unifying beliefs, must include the messaging element of the "toward" vision or solution. What does the group exist for, and how does it help people and rally them to join and make it happen? I got a recent group invite. It is to the Hindu Economic Forum. This community wants to promote businesses owned by Hindus and other Hindu businesses. The vision is to encourage cross-business among the Hindu community to achieve growth. Again, every community has this vision, but it is vital to make it clear and compelling. What will be so persuasive that will inspire you to fight against the forces of power against the "We-group" values?

The successful We-group has a clear vision for that new reality. And here's an important point: ***it cannot be small.*** Group vision must be beyond the vision an individual can achieve. Everyone in the group must feel that only being part of the group helps him attain the vision. The reason is simple. People don't rally to make small things happen. What they rally behind is,

"Oh, wow. This is big. This will make a huge difference in my life and the lives of so many others. I want to get behind this, and I'll sacrifice. I'll work. I'll go out there and spread the word and evangelize because I believe so deeply, and the impact is so potentially big and profound." The group needs to paint a clear picture of that great shared outcome, engaging in every sense. Make it real, and if possible, present tense, as if we've already arrived. Returning to history, many stories of the group standing for a significant cause.

Shivaji is a powerful example of a leader and King who embodied "We-ness" in his approach to influence. During his struggle against the Mughals, Shivaji, even at a young age, didn't just position himself as a lone figure fighting for Swaraj; he consistently emphasized the collective identity of the Hind Swaraj, that is free up from Mughal rule as his vision for a unified nation.

He rooted his vision in the belief that the fight against the Mughals was not just his struggle, but the struggle of all Hindu people. This sense of shared identity and purpose was instrumental in bringing people together across communities and caste divides, ultimately leading to the establishment of the Maratha empire against the mighty forces of the Mughals, who ruled all over India during his time.

Shivaji constantly reminded his cadre that he had that dream and purpose. Shivaji kept moving people to that future state: "This is the mega vision and our path to travel. I have been there, and now we will all go together." Successful businesses must be transparent in that they don't ask the community to just "buy their stuff" but instead make that stuff a reality. If you are thinking small, harnessing people to become buyers, fellow evangelists, and future leaders is nearly impossible.

Apple is making its consumer lives a reality with innovative, secure, and aesthetically designed products. Very often, the better reality is participation in your service, experience, product, business, or brand. Or it is the opportunity to join together, rise, and help you create or grow what everyone needs.

Role of Common Enemy in We-Group

So far, we have talked about who is in and who is out, values, beliefs, and vision, but for the human psyche to connect emotionally, bringing a common enemy becomes critical. Throughout history, a common enemy has often played a pivotal role in uniting groups, whether within a religion, a clan, or a community.

One can observe this phenomenon across various cultures and belief systems. How identifiable this common enemy is, the group has a chance to stand very well. Because as long as a common enemy exists, the group's survival becomes questioned.

Nature reveals, that every animal has developed unique strengths for survival and similarly humans also develop unique strengths to fight and protect their group existence. So, be it in businesses, nations, or sports teams, building a standard enemy narrative plays a critical role in developing the group and sustaining it. Apple identified IBM's big mainframes as a common enemy of visioned PCs in business. Again, the clear identification of IBM as an enemy helped sustain the values and beliefs among Apple employees and, eventually, Apple customers.

Patanjali from Baba Ramdev identified the MNCs and allopathic drug companies as a common enemy for good health and promoted healthy living using Ayurveda. In sports, for example, we had the infamous India-Pakistan as arch-enemies for decades, as well as between England and Australia in cricket. This common enemy raised emotions and made everyone step up with their most significant effort toward winning.

Considering the historical example of cultivating this dynamic comes from the childhood of Shivaji, the revered Maratha leader. Shivaji would play battles with his peers as a boy, dividing them into two groups—one representing Mughal soldiers and the other representing Maratha warriors.

In these mock skirmishes, the Maratha side would always emerge victorious, symbolizing the defeat of the Mughals. This early socialization helped instil a sense of solidarity and collective identity among the Marathas, with the Mughals portrayed as the 'other.' Constructing a common enemy is an effective tool for unity and survival. However, it poses ethical and existential dilemmas when taken too far.

When used in religion or politics, the identifiable common enemy has caused innumerable violence.

So, the challenge lies in finding balance—recognizing the power of unity and acknowledging the potential harm of defining oneself in opposition to others.

That is where the next element of leadership comes in which plays a crucial role in balancing the we-group direction and also growth.

Chapter 7:

Leadership:
Inspiring "We-ness"
in Teams & Communities

Leadership is not about being in charge. It is about taking care of those in your charge."

Simon Sinek

It is very rare to develop We-groups without having a leader. When the systems are in place, and groups have overcome initial setbacks or common enemies, the role of leader might be less required. However, when it comes to formation and creating momentum, leadership becomes critical. But the leadership required here is not the one who stands apart from the crowd, guiding others with their singular brilliance. Instead, it is someone for the sake of "We-ness" who can forge a powerful collective identity that unites people around a common purpose.

We can demonstrate these ideas if we explore how some of history's most influential leaders—ranging from political giants like Winston Churchill, Mahatma Gandhi, and Veer Savarkar to modern-day technologists and business leaders like Warren Buffett—have leveraged "We-ness" to achieve extraordinary influence. Through their stories, we'll uncover key principles that can help you harness the power of collective identity in your leadership journey.

Winston Churchill: The Language of Unity in Times of Crisis

We often remember Winston Churchill as the stoic, unyielding figure who led Britain through its darkest hours during World War II. However, Churchill's success as a leader wasn't just his resolve or strategic insight, but his ability to inspire a sense of "We-ness" among the British during a time of existential threat.

Churchill understood that to rally a nation facing the might have Nazi Germany, he needed to create a collective identity rooted in courage, resilience, and a shared commitment to victory. For him, the common enemy was clear. Hitler and Nazi Germany.

He focused his speeches using language to build "We-ness." Take, for example, his famous address to the House of Commons on June 4, 1940, after the evacuation of Dunkirk: "We shall fight on the beaches, we shall fight on the landing grounds, we shall fight in the fields and the streets, we shall fight in the hills; we shall never surrender."

Churchill's repetition of "we" in this speech wasn't just a rhetorical device; it was a deliberate effort to forge a collective identity. By emphasizing "we" instead of "I" or "you," Churchill placed himself firmly within the collective struggle, reinforcing the idea that victory would be achieved not by individuals but by the united effort of the entire nation. His speeches instilled a sense of shared purpose and resilience, convincing the British people that they were part of a collective that would endure and ultimately triumph. Churchill's leadership during the war was a testament to the power of "We-ness." By creating a narrative of unity and shared destiny, he inspired a beleaguered nation to stand firm against overwhelming odds, and in doing so, he helped to shape the course of history.

Mahatma Gandhi: Non-violence and the Collective Will

Mahatma Gandhi's leadership in India's independence movement is another powerful example of "We-ness" in action. Gandhi didn't just lead a political campaign; he created a mass movement that united millions of Indians across diverse religions, languages, and castes in the struggle for freedom from British rule.

At the heart of Gandhi's approach was *Satyagraha*, or nonviolent resistance. Gandhi understood that to build a successful movement, he needed to create a collective identity that transcended individual differences and empowered ordinary people to participate in the fight for independence. He accomplished this by framing the struggle not as a violent conflict but as a moral crusade based on shared values of truth, justice, and non-violence.

Gandhi's use of "We-ness" was evident in his emphasis on collective action. He encouraged Indians to see themselves as part of a broader community united by a common goal. The Salt March 1930, where Gandhi and his followers walked 240 miles to the Arabian Sea to produce salt in defiance of British law, was a symbolic act of collective resistance. By participating in the march, ordinary Indians became part of a powerful narrative of unity and defiance, reinforcing their shared identity as agents of change. Gandhi's ability to harness "We-ness" was also reflected in his inclusive approach to leadership. He worked tirelessly to ensure that the independence movement represented all Indians, regardless of religion or social status. This inclusivity was vital to the movement's success, allowing millions to see themselves as part of a collective struggle for freedom. Gandhi's leadership demonstrated that "We-ness" can be a powerful force for social change, uniting people around a shared vision and empowering them to take collective action.

Veer Savarkar: The Vision of a United Hindu Nation

Veer Savarkar, a prominent figure in India's struggle for independence, also understood the importance of "We-ness" in uniting people for a common cause. Savarkar was a visionary leader due to his vision of Hindutva—an ideology that emphasized the cultural and national unity of Hindus—which was rooted in creating a strong collective identity. Savarkar understood that to face other united forces, Hindus must become united. We will discuss later on religion how this plays, but here, from a leadership point, we can note that Savarkar's concept of Hindutva wasn't just about religion; it was about forging a sense of national identity based on shared heritage, culture, and values. He believed that a strong, unified identity was essential for resisting colonial rule, Islamic aggression, mass conversions, and building a Hindu sovereign nation.

Through his writings and speeches, Savarkar sought to instil a sense of pride and solidarity among Hindus, encouraging them to see themselves as part of a larger national community. Savarkar's emphasis on "We-ness" was evident in his call for Hindu unity.

He argued that, by embracing a shared identity, Hindus could overcome internal divisions and present a united front against external threats. This focus on collective identity helped to inspire a sense of national consciousness that played a significant role post-India's independence from the rise of the RSS institution and the Bhartiya Janata Party. While Savarkar's legacy is debated, particularly in the context of religious and political divisions in India, his use of "We-ness" as a tool for uniting people around a common cause is undeniable. His leadership highlights the power of collective identity in mobilizing people and shaping national movements.

Warren Buffett: Cultivating a Culture of "We-ness" in Business

In the business world, few leaders exemplify the power of "We-ness" as effectively as Warren Buffett, the legendary investor and CEO of Berkshire Hathaway. Buffett's success isn't just a product of his financial acumen; it's also a result of his ability to build a strong collective identity within his company and among his shareholders.

Buffett's approach to leadership is rooted in trust, transparency, and a shared sense of purpose. He refers to Berkshire Hathaway as a "partnership," emphasizing that he and his shareholders work together towards common goals. This sense of "We-ness" is reinforced by Buffett's annual letters to shareholders, where he shares the company's performance, insights, and plans with remarkable candour.

By treating shareholders as partners, Buffett fosters a collective identity that aligns their interests with the company's long-term success. In one of the annual letters, for a question on what would be advice for shareholders of Berkshire Hathaway for the next 50 years, Buffet says he cannot predict the future. Still, his advice to shareholders is what he would advise his family. Bringing family and equating them to shareholders exemplifies his approach to Unity.

His emphasis on values also characterizes Buffett's leadership style. He frequently speaks about the importance of integrity, patience, and long-term thinking—values he instils in Berkshire Hathaway's corporate culture. By promoting these shared values, Buffett creates a strong sense of "We-ness" among his employees, who see themselves as part of a company that stands for something more than just profits.

Moreover, despite his immense wealth, Buffett's decision to live a relatively modest lifestyle reinforces the idea that he is one of the groups—a partner, not a distant figurehead. This humility and alignment with the values of his shareholders and employees have strengthened the collective identity of Berkshire Hathaway, contributing to its enduring success.

Key Principles for Inspiring "We-ness" as a Leader

The examples of Churchill, Gandhi, Savarkar, and Buffett demonstrate that "We-ness" is a critical component of effective leadership. By creating a strong collective identity, these leaders could inspire and mobilize people, whether during war, social change, or business success. Here are some fundamental principles for inspiring "We-ness" in your leadership:

1. **Align with Shared Values:** To create "We-ness," you must identify and promote values that resonate with your group. These values should reflect the collective identity you want to build and provide a moral compass that guides the group's actions.

2. **Create a Compelling Vision:** A shared vision of the future is essential for building "We-ness." This vision should be aspirational and align with the group's values, providing a sense of purpose that unites people and motivates them to take collective action.

3. **Lead by Example:** To inspire "We-ness," you must embody the values and identity of the group. Leading by example—through actions, lifestyle, or decision-making—demonstrates your commitment to the collective and reinforces the group's identity.

4. **Foster Inclusivity:** "We-ness" thrives in inclusive environments where everyone feels valued and is part of the group. As a leader, ensuring that your group's identity is broad enough to include diverse perspectives and experiences while maintaining a sense of unity is vital.

5. **Communicate Transparently:** Trust is a crucial component of "We-ness." Communicating openly and honestly with your group builds trust and reinforces the idea that everyone works together towards the same goals.

6. **Celebrate Collective Achievements:** Recognizing and celebrating the group's achievements reinforces "We-ness" and strengthens the collective identity. Celebrate not just individual successes but the group's contributions as a whole.

By applying these principles, you can harness the power of "We-ness" to inspire and lead your team, organization, or community. As we continue to explore the concept of "We-ness" in the coming chapters, let us look at how language plays a big role.

Chapter 8:

The Art of Shared Language: How Words Create "We-ness"

"Words are, of course, the most powerful drug used by mankind."

Rudyard Kipling

Just think about words such as Lawyer, Doctor, Love, God, or Peace. These words do not have a single definition or expression. Ask ten people; their definition reveals their beliefs, experiences, stories, and knowledge. So, words matter. They shape our thoughts, influence our emotions, and, ultimately, define our reality. In the context of "We-ness," language isn't just a tool for communication—it's the glue that binds a group together. Let's now explore the power of a shared language in building "We-ness." We'll look at how words, phrases, and narratives forge group identity, drawing on historical lessons and contemporary business examples to illustrate language's critical role in influencing and uniting people.

The Power of Language in Shaping Identity

The language creates and reinforces collective identity, signalling who belongs and doesn't and what's valued and what's not. Through language, we articulate our shared values, beliefs, goals, and experiences, transforming a collection of individuals into a cohesive "We." In a group context, shared language creates a sense of unity and belonging, making it clear that we're part of something larger than ourselves. Let's go back to a few millennia and consider the role of language in the life of Buddha. Buddha, after realization, wished to reach the masses. Buddha understood that the best way to teach his findings is in a language the common man can understand. Hence, they taught the teachings of Buddha, Dhamma, and Sangha in the local Prakrit language instead of Sanskrit, which only elites spoke then. So, Buddha gained wider acceptance as the language helped reach everyone. Similarly, in any social or political movement, influential leaders like PM Narendra Modi's political speeches aren't just influential because of their rhetorical skill; they are powerful because they use language to articulate a collective vision that unites their followers toward a shared future.

Phrases like Jan–Jan Modi, Ghar-Ghar Modi, Abki Baar Modi Sarkar ("Time for Change, Time for Modi.") became rallying cries that united people across geographic divides. These words didn't just describe a movement—they defined it, creating a shared identity among a section of voters that was crucial to its success. Similarly, the catchphrase of MAGA, Make America Great Again by Trump, created a movement. Everyone could identify those who subscribe to MAGA as part of Trump's supporting community. Even consider some of the social movements like the civil rights movement. Dr. Martin Luther King Jr.'s speeches weren't just powerful because of their rhetorical skill; they were powerful because they used language to articulate a collective vision of equality and justice. Phrases like "I have a dream" and "Let freedom ring" became rallying cries that united people across racial and geographic divides. These words didn't just describe desire but created a movement—creating a shared identity crucial to its success.

Creating "We-ness" Through Language in Businesses

Language's role in fostering unity is not just in politics or activism. It plays an equally powerful role in contemporary business. Studies show that top consumer-facing companies always ensure that they successfully build strong cultures and brand communities that understand the importance of shared language.

Take Starbucks, for example. The company has created a unique lexicon that extends beyond the coffee menu. Terms like "barista," "venti," and "Frappuccino" aren't just product names; they're part of a shared language that reinforces the Starbucks experience. When customers order a "grande latte" instead of a medium, they're not just making a purchase—they're participating in a shared culture that distinguishes them as members of the Starbucks community.

It starts with developing a shared vocabulary—a set of words and phrases with specific meanings within the group. This vocabulary becomes a code that signals membership and reinforces group identity. You are signalling that you belong when you speak the group's language. Let's look at an example from the tech world again: Apple. Apple crafts its product names and marketing language carefully to create a sense of exclusivity and innovation. The company's use of the prefix "i" in products like the iPhone, iPad, and iMac isn't just a branding choice—it's a linguistic tool that reinforces the idea of a personal, individual experience within a larger Apple community. The language Apple uses in its marketing—terms like "revolutionary," "magical," and "it just works"—also contributes to the collective identity of Apple users as part of a forward-thinking, cutting-edge group.

This use of language to create "We-ness" isn't limited to product names and slogans. Internal communication also plays a critical role in shaping collective identity in business. Companies that cultivate strong cultures develop internal lexicons that reflect their values and priorities. For example, at Google, "Googler" refers to employees, while "Noogler" refers to new hires. These terms aren't just playful nicknames; they're part of a shared language that reinforces the collective identity of Google employees and their connection to the company's culture.

Shared language also plays a crucial role in maintaining group cohesion over time. As groups grow and evolve, their language evolves, adapting to new challenges, opportunities, and experiences. This ongoing language development helps keep the group's identity fresh and relevant, ensuring that the sense of "We-ness" remains strong.

Language as a Tool for Inclusion and Exclusion

One of the most potent aspects of shared language is its ability to include or exclude. When you know the language of a group, you are in—you are part of the "We." But when you don't know the language, you are on the outside, unable to fully participate in the group's identity and culture.

We can see dynamics in both historical and contemporary contexts. In ancient India, Sanskrit was the language of power and culture. To be fluent in Sanskrit, one had to be part of the priest-brahmin and ruling classes. Those who spoke other languages often missed the latest developments and wisdom. Language was a marker of identity and status, defining who belonged and who didn't. A similar thing existed in ancient Rome; Latin was the language of power and culture. To be fluent in Latin was to be part of the elite, the ruling class. They marginalized those who spoke other languages and were seen as "barbarians" outside the civilized world.

Fast forward to the present, and we see similar dynamics in the corporate world. In many companies, a specialized jargon or set of acronyms develops over time. This internal language can be a powerful tool for building "We-ness" among employees, creating a sense of shared knowledge and expertise. However, it can also create barriers for newcomers or outsiders who aren't yet familiar with the language.

In 1997, as a fresher, I joined Motorola. The group I joined already had quite a few experienced members. I was one of 2 recruits who joined as fresh out of college. In the initial few months, I faced a big challenge, not because of technical issues but because the experienced team had created so much jargon and language that in many meetings and lunches, I just kept quiet, listening, and trying to understand.

Finally, a senior two years ahead of me understood my challenge, taught me most of the group vocabulary, and helped me start joining the discussions. This is why onboarding processes that include language orientation are so important—they help new employees learn the "language" of the company, allowing them to integrate more fully into the group.

Language can also be a tool for the exclusion of less apparent ways. Consider the use of gendered language in the workplace. With more women in the workforce, older phrases like "manpower" or "chairman" are no longer encouraged as they subtly reinforce male dominance in a way that can alienate women. By contrast, using more inclusive language—such as "workforce" or "chairperson"—can help to create a more inclusive and cohesive collective identity.

In branding, the companies use language to create a sense of exclusivity that appeals to specific audiences while excluding others. For example, luxury brands like Rolex or Louis Vuitton use language that emphasizes exclusivity, quality, and status. The words and phrases associated with these brands create a sense of "We-ness" among their customers—an elite group that sets itself apart from the masses.

Crafting a Language of Success in Business

In the business world, companies that understand the power of language to create "We-ness" often build the strongest brands and cultures. These companies don't just sell products or services; they sell an identity—a way of communication through carefully crafted language.

Consider Airbnb, the online marketplace for short-term lodging. From its inception, Airbnb has used language to create a sense of community among hosts and guests. The company's "Belong Anywhere" tagline isn't just a marketing slogan; it's a statement of shared values that speaks to a global community where everyone can feel at home.

Airbnb's use of language also extends to its internal culture, where employees are encouraged to see themselves as part of a mission to create a world where anyone can "Belong Anywhere." This shared language has been instrumental in building a robust and cohesive culture that unites employees, hosts, and guests with a common identity.

Another powerful example is Nike, which has long mastered using language to build "We-ness." Nike's famous slogan, "Just Do It," is more than just an encouragement to buy shoes; it's a call to action that resonates with athletes and aspirants worldwide.

The simplicity and directness of the phrase make it universally relatable. At the same time, its association with Nike creates a strong brand identity that unites consumers in a shared belief in perseverance, determination, and achievement. When someone wears Nike gear, they're not just wearing a product—they're making a statement about their values and identity as part of the Nike community.

Crafting Your Language of "We-ness"

The examples we've explored show how powerful shared language can be in creating and sustaining "We-ness." But how can you apply these principles to build a strong collective identity in your group, organization, or community? Here are some strategies to consider:

1. **Develop a Shared Vocabulary:** Identify keywords and phrases that reflect your group's values and goals. These could be terms that describe your mission, culture, or your identity's unique aspects. Use this vocabulary consistently in your communication to reinforce the group's identity.

2. **Use language Inclusively:** Pay attention to your language and its impact on different group members. Strive to use inclusive language that reflects the diversity of your group and makes everyone feel welcome and valued.

3. **Evolve Your Language Over Time:** As your group grows and evolves, so should your language. Be open to adapting your vocabulary and narrative to reflect new experiences, challenges, and opportunities. This flexibility ensures that your "We-ness" remains relevant and dynamic.

Chapter 9:

The Role of Rituals & Symbols in Cementing Identity

Rituals keep us connected to our roots.

Anonymous

Rituals are the repeated actions, ceremonies, and traditions that give life to a group's identity. They provide continuity, create a sense of belonging, and help to internalize the group's values.

Now, most people think rituals are related to religion. However, as you can see in this chapter, one of the core elements of keeping the "we-group" together is through common rituals. These rituals aren't just for show; they're powerful psychological tools that reinforce the group's cohesion and world of sports. Today, most teams have embedded certain rituals in the pre-game or middle of the games.

Take the pre-game ritual of haka performed by New Zealand's All Blacks rugby team or the synchronized handshakes of US NBA players—serve to unify the team, mentally prepare them for competition, and remind them of their collective identity.

In a corporate context, rituals can include annual retreats, company-wide meetings, or even daily stand-ups where team members come together to share updates and reaffirm their commitment to the group's goals. These rituals help to maintain a strong sense of "We-ness" within the organization, ensuring that employees remain aligned with the company's values and objectives.

Rituals also play a significant role in customer-facing brands. Consider Harley-Davidson, the iconic motorcycle company. Harley owners don't just buy a bike; they become part of a lifestyle. I have a friend who is a Harley owner in the US. He regularly attends the annual Sturgis Motorcycle Rally, where thousands of Harley riders converge, which cements the brand's collective identity. It's a celebration of the values of freedom, rebellion, and camaraderie that define the Harley community.

Rituals are essential because they create a sense of continuity and tradition. They link the past with the present, providing a shared history that strengthens the group's identity. When members participate in rituals, they're not just engaging in a routine; they're reaffirming their place in the "We" and reinforcing the bonds that hold the group together.

Symbols as Anchors of Collective Identity

Just as rituals breathe life into collective identity, Symbols have long been a powerful tool for leaders seeking to create a sense of unity and collective identity and act as anchors. Symbols are the visual, auditory, and even tactile representations of a group's values and goals. From ancient empires to modern-day businesses, symbols represent a group's values, beliefs, and aspirations. They provide a focal point for collective identity, encapsulating complex ideas in simple, memorable forms that can inspire loyalty, solidarity, and even action.

They are the flags we wave, the logos we wear, the anthems we sing. Symbols distil complex ideas into simple, powerful images or sounds that can instantly evoke the group's identity and everything it stands for. Think of the power of national flags. In the corporate world, logos function similarly. The Indian flag, for example, isn't just a piece of cloth; it's a symbol of freedom, democracy, diversity, and the shared history of India. For millions of Indians, the flag represents a collective identity, transcending individual differences. This transcending symbolic power is so potent that it can evoke deep emotions and even inspire people to action—whether it's fighting for the country in times of war or advocating for social justice under the banner of that same flag.

Symbols are particularly effective because they operate on both a conscious and subconscious level. Consciously, we recognize and interpret symbols based on their visual characteristics and the meanings we associate with them. Subconsciously, symbols can evoke emotions and memories that reinforce our connection to the group. Hence, we use symbols in branding, marketing, and social movements—they're a shortcut to the heart, capable of encapsulating and conveying a group's identity in a single image or sound.

Let's explore, throughout history, how they used the symbols to reinforce a sense of "We-ness." We'll examine this practice's positive and negative aspects, drawing on examples from ancient empires, totalitarian regimes, and modern businesses. By understanding the power of symbols, we can learn to use them more thoughtfully and ethically in our leadership and organizational contexts.

The Power of Symbols in Ancient Empires

Symbols have been central to the governance and unity of empires since the dawn of civilization. Ancient leaders understood that to govern vast territories with diverse populations, they needed to create a shared sense of identity among their subjects. Symbols, rituals, and monuments were vital in achieving this goal.

One of the most iconic examples is the Roman Empire, which used the eagle (*Aquila*) to symbolize its power and unity. The Roman legions carried the eagle on standards, and it was a potent symbol of Rome's military might and divine favour. Wherever the Roman legions marched, the eagle standard went with them, a constant reminder to Romans and conquered peoples of the empire's strength and authority. The eagle represented the emperor's power and served as a unifying symbol for the diverse peoples within the empire, helping to forge a collective identity under Roman rule.

The wheel symbol of the Indian flag is called Dharma chakra, or Dharma Wheel. The Dharma chakra is the most important symbol of Buddhism. It represents the Buddha's first sermon at Sarnath, which marked the beginning of Buddhist Law. The wheel also represents the completeness of the Dharma and the connection between the steps of the Eight-Fold Path.

Figure 2: Worshipers and Dharmachakra, Sanchi Stupa, South Face, West Pillar.

So, the symbols were not just decorative; they were powerful tools for communicating complex ideas and values that resonated deeply with people's emotions and beliefs. By creating and disseminating these symbols, ancient leaders were able to build and maintain a sense of "We-ness" that was crucial to the stability and cohesion of their empires.

Hitler and the Swastika

While symbols can unite people around positive ideals, they also act as weapons to propagate division. One of the most infamous examples of this is Adolf Hitler's use of the swastika during the rise of Nazi Germany.

The swastika, an ancient symbol used in Hindu cultures as a sign of good fortune and prosperity, was appropriated by Hitler and the Nazi Party in the 1920s.

The swastika's ubiquity and the Nazi regime's relentless use of propaganda helped to create a strong sense of "We-ness" among those who identified with Hitler's vision for Germany. It became a rallying point for millions of Germans, who drew into a collective identity that justified hatred, violence, and genocide.

The swastika's power as a symbol was not just in its visual impact but in the way, it encapsulated the core beliefs of the Nazi regime, creating a clear distinction between those who were part of the "We" (the so-called Aryan race) and those who were the "Other" (Jews, Roma, and other marginalized groups).

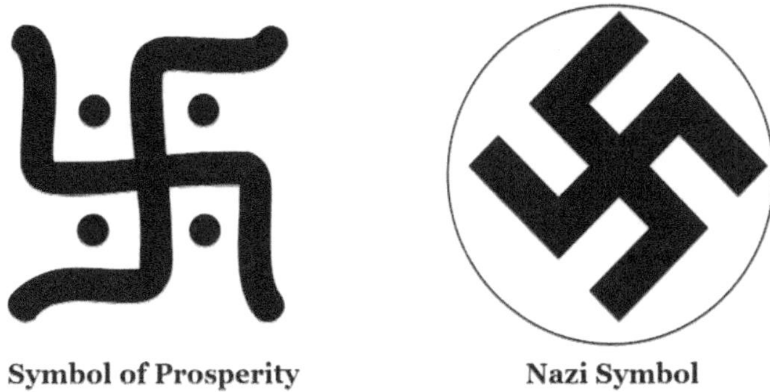

Symbol of Prosperity   **Nazi Symbol**

Figure 3: Swastika symbol of Hindu vs Nazi

Hitler's use of the swastika demonstrates the dark potential of symbols when they are used to manipulate and control. It is a cautionary tale about the ethical responsibility of using symbols to create and reinforce collective identity. When bad actors wield symbols, they can lead to devastating consequences, perpetuating division, violence, and suffering on an unimaginable scale.

Creating Brand Unity in Businesses

In business, symbols are crucial in creating a sense of unity and loyalty among customers and employees. A potent brand symbol can encapsulate a company's identity, values, and mission, serving as a rallying point for internal and external stakeholders. When used effectively, these symbols can foster a powerful sense of "We-ness" that drives brand loyalty, employee engagement, and overall success.

One of the most successful examples of this is Apple's iconic logo—a simple, sleek apple with a bite taken out of it. The Apple logo is more than just a symbol of the company; it represents a philosophy of innovation, creativity, and user-centric design.

For millions of customers worldwide, the Apple logo symbolizes cutting-edge technology and high-quality products that make their lives easier and more enjoyable. This strong brand identity has created a loyal following, with customers who feel deeply connected to the Apple brand, often identifying as part of the Apple community.

Apple's use of symbols extends beyond its logo. The design of its products, the minimalist aesthetic of its retail stores, and even its marketing campaigns all reinforce the company's brand identity. For example, the iconic "Think Different" campaign of the late 1990s used images of visionary figures like Albert Einstein, Martin Luther King Jr., and Mahatma Gandhi, coupled with the Apple logo, to create a powerful narrative of innovation and change. This campaign attracted customers and created a sense of pride and unity among Apple employees, who saw themselves as part of a company that was changing the world.

Another example is Nike's "swoosh" logo, recognized globally as a symbol of athleticism, performance, and empowerment. The swoosh, the company's "Just Do It" slogan, has become synonymous with Nike's brand identity, inspiring millions of athletes and fitness enthusiasts worldwide.

The simplicity of the swoosh, combined with its dynamic design, conveys a sense of movement and progress, aligning perfectly with Nike's mission to empower people to push their limits and achieve their goals. This symbol has helped to create a strong sense of "We-ness" among Nike customers, who identify with the brand's values and see themselves as part of a larger community of athletes.

Harnessing the Power of Symbols for Positive "We-ness"

Symbols are a powerful tool for creating and reinforcing "We-ness." When used thoughtfully and ethically, they can unite people around a shared identity, inspire loyalty and pride, and drive collective action. Whether in ancient empires, modern businesses, or organizational cultures, symbols can encapsulate complex ideas and values in a way that resonates deeply with people's emotions and beliefs.

Symbols can evoke strong emotions and shape collective identity, so it's essential to consider their impact on the group and the broader society. One key consideration is the inclusivity of the symbol. Leaders should choose symbols that reflect the group's diversity and resonate with many people. Too narrow or exclusionary symbols can alienate group members or create divisions, undermining the sense of "We-ness" that the leader is trying to build. However, the power of symbols also comes with responsibility. Leaders must use symbols with care, ensuring that they promote inclusivity, authenticity, and ethical behaviour. By doing so, they can harness the positive potential of symbols to create strong, cohesive communities united by a shared sense of purpose and identity.

Chapter 10:

Stories That Unite: The Role of Narrative in Building Influence

After nourishment, shelter, and companionship, stories are what we need most in the world."

Philip Pullman

Now, we are in the final element of "We-ness". It is about the stories, one of the most critical elements to create the bond, and it is often overlooked by many. But as you will understand in this chapter, humans are storytelling creatures.

If unity serves our tribal natures, stories do more than just entertain; they bind us together, shaping our collective identity and driving collective action.

From the earliest days of sitting around campfires to the modern-day phenomenon of binge-watching Netflix, stories have been the primary way we make sense of the world, connect with others, and understand our place in a larger collective.

In this chapter, we'll explore the power of how the narrative in creating and sustaining "We-ness." Again, we'll dive into some historical examples where the right story has united empires and armies, and we'll look at contemporary stories in businesses and other cultural phenomena that demonstrate how powerful narratives can forge deep connections among people.

The Power of Narrative in Shaping Collective Identity

Stories are particularly compelling in sustaining the "We-ness" because they engage our brains' rational and emotional aspects. They provide logical coherence—explaining why the group exists, what it stands for, and what it aims to achieve—while also evoking emotions that strengthen our attachment to the group. This dual impact makes stories critical in building and sustaining collective identity.

Narrative is the thread that weaves together the fabric of "We-ness." Through stories, we understand who we are as a group, what we value, and what we strive for. Stories provide context, meaning, and continuity, transforming abstract concepts like "unity" or "purpose" into tangible, relatable experiences.

I recently learned that what we see, whether history, politics or even social circle, is all about snapshots. It means a few minutes of information or some content, but our brain builds a narrative or story to complete this snapshot.

The kind of story we build around the snapshot we see depends again on one's beliefs, values, and identity they carry. Stories about the company's founding, key milestones, or legendary employees become part of the organizational culture in a workplace. These stories are passed down, celebrated, and even mythologized, helping to create a shared history and identity with which new employees can connect.

Stories of individual courage, collective action, and hard-won victories inspire and motivate members of social movements. In every nation, there are stories of fighters and wars that shape the nation's history. In India, the stories of the 1857 freedom movement or Bhagat Singh, who at the age of 22 rebelled against the British establishment and was hanged to death, are not just historical accounts; they're foundational narratives that continue to shape the collective identity of the revolutionary movement and its ongoing freedom struggles.

Sports teams have stories of losses, victors, eventful matches, and comeback stories. Who in India doesn't remember the cricket team's World Cup victory in 1983 or 2011? It is etched in the memory of every cricket fan. Or, for that matter, when it comes to football, I remember Argentina's world cup victory in 1986 and the rise of Maradona; It is something many Argentinians recollect.

To get more into this, first, I like to explore how stories built and held empires together. Consider the story of the Maurya Empire, one of the most powerful empires in Indian history. The narrative of the Maurya empire wasn't just about conquest and power; it was about the idea of "Akhand Bharat" itself—a symbol of civilization, law, and order.

Chanakya, a tutor and guide who helped to found this empire, believed that it was the duty to connect Bharath to one nation and safeguard it from external enemies. Bring back the order of law and fairness. This narrative wasn't just propaganda; it was a shared belief that united the diverse peoples of the empire, from Central India to North and even Western India to Afghanistan.

The story of Bharat as the Akhanda, the heart of a vast and enduring empire, created a powerful sense of "We-ness" among its citizens, soldiers, and allies, which helped maintain its dominance for centuries. Similarly, consider the story of the Roman Empire, one of the most powerful empires in history. Again, the narrative of Rome wasn't just about conquest and power; it was about the idea of "Rome" itself—a symbol of civilization, law, and order.

Romans believed they were the bearers of a divine destiny to bring peace and prosperity to the world through the "Pax Romana," or Roman Peace. This narrative wasn't just propaganda; it was a shared belief that united the diverse peoples of the empire, from the British Isles to the deserts of Africa.

The story of Rome as the eternal city, the heart of a vast and enduring empire, created a powerful sense of "We-ness" among its citizens, soldiers, and allies, which helped maintain its dominance for centuries. During the Indian freedom movement, the citizens of India united around the narrative of fighting against the British Raj. Again, this story wasn't just a justification for the fight; it was a mighty rallying cry to fight against colonial power that brought together society with different cultures, languages, castes, religions, and interests.

The narrative of the "Freedom Fighters," those who fought and sacrificed during the Indian freedom struggle, became a defining story of collective identity for decades across India. This shared story continues to influence our national identity, values, and even policies today.

The Science of Stories: Why They Work

Why are stories so effective at creating "We-ness"? The answer lies in the way our brains process information. Neuroscientists have found that stories light up more parts of our brains than simple facts or statements.

When listening to stories, neurons in our brain fire in the same patterns as the speaker's, a process known as "neural coupling", also called as mirroring. So, our brains simulate the experiences described, creating a sense of empathy and connection. This makes stories particularly effective at building emotional bonds and shared identity.

Furthermore, stories can simplify complex ideas and make them more relatable. Clear narratives cut through distractions. Stories help us pay attention–particularly in this attention era when vying for people's focus is more coveted than ever. Imagine when watching a movie or watching a dram, you are not just processing information; you are experiencing emotions, imagining scenarios, and connecting the narrative to our lives. This process helps to embed the story—and the collective identity it represents—deeply into our consciousness.

In a group context, stories provide a shared experience that unites people, even from different backgrounds or perspectives.

It is why stories are a powerful tool for anyone looking to build and sustain "We-ness." Crafting a compelling narrative can create a sense of unity and purpose that drives collective action.

Contemporary Business Stories: Building Brands Through Narrative

In the business world, companies that understand the power of storytelling often build the strongest brands and most loyal customer bases. These companies don't just sell products or services; they sell stories—narratives that resonate with their customers' values, aspirations, and identities.

Consider the example of **Bajaj Auto**, a brand integral to India's automotive landscape since the 1970s. Bajaj's storytelling goes far beyond its motorcycles and scooters—it's about freedom, empowerment, and the spirit of self-reliance. Bajaj's iconic campaigns have told stories that resonate with the aspirations of millions of Indians, making the brand synonymous with personal progress and the road to independence.

One of Bajaj's most memorable campaigns is the "Hamara Bajaj" campaign, which struck a deep chord with the Indian public. The ad was more than just about scooters; it celebrated Indian pride, tradition, and the spirit of moving forward. "Hamara Bajaj" symbolized the dreams and ambitions of middle-class families, reflecting their desire for upward mobility and independence. It was not just about owning a scooter—it was about owning a symbol of progress. This narrative of empowerment through mobility is what made Bajaj a household name.

Bajaj continues to tell stories that reflect the evolving aspirations of Indians. With products like Pulsar, and the Dominar motorcycles, the company shifted its storytelling to focus on adventure, freedom, and the thrill of the open road. These narratives speak to a younger, more dynamic audience that seeks self-expression and exploration. The Pulsar's campaigns often feature riders pushing boundaries, exploring new terrains, and embodying a fearless attitude. Through these stories, Bajaj has built a strong emotional connection with its audience, who see the brand as enabling their freedom and adventures.

Moreover, Bajaj's storytelling extends to its role in India's economic and industrial growth. As a brand that has played a vital role in shaping India's automotive industry, Bajaj tells a story of innovation, resilience, and a commitment to the nation's development. This narrative reinforces Bajaj's identity as a modern brand and is rooted in the values of hard work and progress.

Through its storytelling, Bajaj Auto has created a deep sense of "We-ness" among its customers—a collective identity of pride, freedom, and forward momentum. When customers buy a Bajaj vehicle, they're not just purchasing a mode of transport—they're buying into a legacy of empowerment and progress that has touched the lives of millions across India.

Consider the example of **Zomato**, one of India's leading food delivery platforms. Zomato's success lies not only in its seamless service but in its ability to tell stories that resonate with the everyday lives of its users. Their marketing isn't just about convenience and food delivery—it's about the emotions, quirks, and experiences that revolve around food in the modern Indian lifestyle.

Zomato's social media campaigns are a masterclass in relatable, witty storytelling. Whether it's a light-hearted post about midnight cravings, an amusing take on dealing with unpredictable weather, or playful interactions around cricket matches, Zomato creates stories that reflect the daily lives of its users. For example, during the lockdown, Zomato's clever messaging highlighted the comfort food brings in uncertain times, making customers feel understood and connected to a larger community of food lovers. These stories are not just ads—they reflect moments everyone can identify with, making Zomato a part of its users' everyday narratives.

Zomato also tells stories of empowerment and convenience. From enabling small restaurants to reach larger audiences to helping customers discover new cuisines, Zomato's platform positions itself as more than just a food delivery service. This community brings together people with diverse tastes and preferences. The company's campaigns often feature relatable, everyday characters—students ordering pizza during late-night study sessions, professionals looking for quick meal options, or families enjoying Sunday brunch. These scenarios make the brand feel indispensable to its users' lives.

By consistently telling stories that reflect the modern Indian lifestyle, Zomato has built a strong "We-ness" among its users. It's not just a service; it's part of a shared cultural experience of food, convenience, and joy. When users open the Zomato app, they're not just ordering food but connecting to a larger narrative of shared moments, humour, and community.

Another powerful example that connects to higher values is the traditional clothing company FabIndia.

FabIndia's narrative is around traditional craftsmanship and the idea that business can be a force for good. The company tells stories of how local traditions and Indian dressing sense align with its customers' values. This narrative isn't just marketing; it reflects FabIndia's mission and identity.

By consistently telling this story, FabIndia has built a strong "We-ness" among its customers, employees, and partners—a community united by a shared commitment to protecting the Indian dressing sense.

Crafting the Narrative of "We-ness"

Suppose you want to rally people to some kind of cause, whether non-consumer or consumer, social. Building a powerful shared story is necessary. You need to ask what the brand's story is and what the story is that one wants to make the We-ness around. There are many stories, but symbols follow and connect with core values and beliefs to keep the ritual going. The story is the glue that connects.

Stories will have pain, suffering, and victory, though you may not even know you are in it yet. The actors in the story go through inciting incidents, are reluctant, and eventually cross the threshold, and the journey gets rolling. Actors face tests, gain allies, meet mentors, face an ordeal, find the elixir/ salvation, become resurrected, and then return home to share what they have learned and mentor others.

In sharing that story, one simultaneously tells the story of everyone they would like to move into this group. With a well-narrated story, it transports the listeners into it.

The story becomes what David Gordon called a therapeutic metaphor. Stories create a powerful state of deep connection and resonance. And, of course, whatever story you tell must be based on the truth. You never make stuff up; you just learn how to tell the story most compellingly.

Understanding the power of narrative is one thing; crafting your own compelling story of "We-ness" is another. Whether leading a team, building a brand, or organizing a community, the proper narrative can be a powerful tool for creating and sustaining collective identity.

Here are some strategies to consider:

1. **Identify Your Core Values:** Identify the core values defining your group or organization. These values will form the foundation of your narrative, guiding the stories you tell and the identity you create.

2. **Create a Vision of the Future:** A powerful narrative often includes a vision of the future—a story about what your group strives to achieve. This vision should be inspiring, aspirational, and aligned with your core values. It's the "why" behind your actions and the glue that holds your group together.

3. **Tell Stories of Struggle and Triumph:** Stories of overcoming challenges and achieving success are particularly effective at building "We-ness." These narratives resonate with people on an emotional level, creating a sense of shared experience and collective

identity. Highlight your group's struggles and the victories you've achieved together.

4. **Use Symbols and Language to Reinforce Your Narrative:** As discussed in the previous chapter, symbols and language are powerful tools for reinforcing your narrative. Use them consistently to create a cohesive story that resonates with your group and strengthens your collective identity.

5. **Evolve Your Narrative Over Time:** As your group grows and evolves, so should your narrative. Be open to adapting your story to reflect new experiences, challenges, and goals. This flexibility ensures your narrative remains relevant and engaging, keeping your "We-ness" strong.

By crafting and sharing a compelling narrative, you can create a powerful sense of "We-ness" that unites people around a common identity and purpose. As we explore "We-ness" in the coming chapters, we will explore how these principles apply in various contexts, from leadership and marketing to social movements and cultural change.

PART III

OBSERVING WE-NESS EVERYWHERE

Chapter 11:

From "Me" to "We": How Social Media Shapes Collective Identity

"Social media is about sociology and psychology more than technology."

Brian Solis

In today's hyper-connected world, social media has become a powerful force in shaping collective identity. Platforms like Instagram, TikTok, Twitter, WhatsApp, YouTube, and Facebook aren't just tools for communication; they serve as digital spaces where modern tribes form and cultivate "We-ness" on a massive scale.

This phenomenon starts with teenagers using social media to explore their identities, connect with peers, and find their place in a larger community. However, while social media can foster a sense of belonging and unity, it has a darker side, with significant risks and harmful effects. Let's explore how social media pulls the globe into "We-ness" and examine this shift's positive and negative implications. How can parents, educators, and leaders navigate this digital landscape?

The Allure of "We-ness" in the Digital Age

The transition from childhood to teenage is a critical period of identity formation. It's a time when kids seek to define who they are, where they belong, and how they fit into the world.

When I was growing up, I came from a large family of 5 brothers and one sister, and we lived in a locality where I had a large circle of friends. Now, through parents, friends watching TV, and reading books, we all had that helped answer the above questions. But today, social media offers an immediate and compelling way to explore the questions. It provides a platform for self-expression, connection, and validation, making it a natural environment for young adults to cultivate a sense of "We-ness."

One of the critical ways' social media fosters "We-ness" is through creating online communities. These communities often revolve around shared interests, values, or experiences—whether it's a fandom for a particular artist, a shared commitment to a social cause, or participation in a viral trend. COVID virtually locked us down, and I experienced the force of digital communities first-hand. I gave my daughter access to a laptop and mobile phone for hours at a remote school. She was in the 5th standard. I saw a shift in her behaviour from shopping requests, new words she picked up, and her interest in strange music. I had no idea where she was getting ideas, but later, I learned she had gotten hooked on Korean fandoms, such as those for BTS or BLACKPINK, which have millions of members worldwide.

These fans, known as "ARMY" for BTS or "Blinks" for BLACKPINK, share a love for the music and a collective identity reinforced through social media interactions. She started using hashtags to create fan art and engage in coordinated efforts like streaming music videos or voting in polls to strengthen their sense of belonging to that community. She has moved on, but many in her circle have these strong identities of "ARMY' & "Blinks."

Another powerful example is the rise of social justice movements on platforms like Instagram and Twitter. Have you come across sudden movements that have risen, such as #DEI, #FridaysForFuture, #Wokeness, and #MeToo that aim to mobilize millions of young people worldwide? Through these movements, teens or young adults won't just become passive observers but active participants in shaping the narrative and driving change. Again, hashtags, retweets, and viral challenges all aimed to allow them to contribute to a collective voice that demands attention and action. Digital activism fosters a strong sense of 'We-ness' as young people unite to fight for causes they believe in or are led to believe, often transcending geographical and cultural boundaries.

The Positive Force of Digital "We-ness"

Creating and participating in online communities can have significant positive effects. For many, social media provides a sense of connection and support they might not find in their immediate offline environment. It is particularly true for teens who feel isolated, with both parents busy or other factors, such as being part of their community. Online communities can sometimes offer a safe space to express themselves, find like-minded peers, and build confidence in their identity. There are many apps today that create communities. Let's take Starmaker, an app that caters to music lovers. The app allows the subscribers to become part of the tribe and form virtual family support groups to encourage people to become part of their small communities. Organizers hold competitions, and each group engages like real-world communities to support their members.

Similarly, people interested in gaming often find themselves in online communities where they connect and share their skills and experiences. Platforms like Reddit are creating ways to form groups that become vital spaces for tribe members to share their stories, seek advice, and form supportive networks. This creative participation often leads to the forming of subcultures or "tribes" that are united by a shared aesthetic or interest. These subcultures provide a sense of identity and belonging that is reinforced through the continuous exchange of content and ideas.

The Dark Side of Digital "We-ness": Harmful Effects and Risks

While the digital world offers many opportunities for building "We-ness," it also comes with significant risks. The very features that make social media so appealing—its immediacy, reach, and capacity for connection—can also lead to harmful consequences.

One of the most concerning aspects of digital "We-ness" is the potential for groupthink and echo chambers. Online communities bring like-minded individuals together, often amplifying ideas without much critical examination. They are often leading to the reinforcement of harmful beliefs or behaviours. For example, toxic subcultures form around harmful practices such as cyberbullying, shaming, or radical political ideologies. In these environments, often silencing the dissenting voices, the group's norms become increasingly extreme, leading to a distorted sense of reality and reinforcing unhealthy behaviours.

The anonymity and distance provided by the internet also contribute to negative behaviour. The collective identity formed in certain online groups gives rise to a "mob mentality," where individuals feel emboldened to act in ways they wouldn't in face-to-face interactions. This results in significant psychological harm for those targeted, leading to anxiety, depression, and even suicidal thoughts.

Another harmful effect of digital "We-ness" is the pressure to conform. Social media platforms often reward content that aligns with popular trends or norms through likes, shares, or algorithmic promotion. It creates intense pressure to fit in and present a curated version of oneself that conforms to the expectations of their online community. The constant comparison to others' seemingly perfect lives is, in a way, leading to issues like low self-esteem, anxiety, and a distorted self-image.

Moreover, the addictive nature of social media exacerbates these issues. The need for validation through likes and comments often leads to compulsive use, with many spending hours each day on their devices, often at the expense of real-world relationships and activities. This overreliance on social media for social interaction ultimately contributes to feelings of loneliness and isolation, ironically undermining the sense of "We-ness" that individuals from teens to adults seek.

Navigating the Complexities of Digital "We-ness"

Given the powerful influence of social media on teens' collective identity, it's becoming crucial to find ways to navigate this complex landscape. While the goal isn't to eliminate social media use or censor everything—given its pervasive role in modern life—here are some ways that, if practised, will help.

1. **Media Literacy:** The ability to critically evaluate online content is essential. It includes understanding how algorithms work, recognizing bias, and questioning the validity of information. Media literacy empowers one to think critically about the online communities we engage with and the narratives we encounter, helping to avoid echo chambers and harmful group dynamics.

2. **Foster Positive Online Communities:** Especially when it comes to teens, instead of trying to keep teens off social media altogether, it's more productive to help them find and engage with positive online communities. It could involve connecting with groups that share their interests in a healthy, supportive way or participating in digital activism that aligns with their values. Encouraging community participation that promotes positivity, creativity, and inclusivity will help reinforce a healthy sense of "We-ness."

3. **Being role models:** As parents and educators, one can set an example by modelling own behaviour. It includes being mindful of one's social media use, engaging in respectful online discussions, and prioritizing real-world relationships. By demonstrating how to use social

media responsibly and constructively, adults can help teens develop similar habits.

4. **Support Mental Health:** Recognizing social media's potential mental health impacts is crucial. Giving access to mental health resources and encouraging open conversations about their online experiences in a way helps mitigate the adverse effects. Teens need to know they can seek help if they feel overwhelmed or distressed by social media interactions.

5. **Encourage Self-Expression Beyond Social Media:** While social media is a powerful tool for self-expression, it shouldn't be the only outlet. Encouraging teens to explore their identities through other means—such as art, writing, sports, or community involvement—will help them develop a more balanced sense of self that isn't solely dependent on online validation.

Chapter 12:

The Dark Side of "We-ness": When Unity Becomes Dangerous

You need to force yourself to consider opposing arguments, especially when they challenge the core ideas of your investment thesis.

Charlie Munger

"So far, we explored the power of unity and how 'We-ness' unites people, fosters cooperation, and drives collective action as a powerful force for good. In this chapter, I will share a few examples of its dark side and how some misuse it for harmful purposes." When manipulated by bad actors or taken to extremes, the same sense of unity that brings people together can lead to harmful behaviours, the protection of wrongdoers, and the perpetuation of destructive ideologies.

Let's examine how cult leaders, criminal organizations, and other groups exploit 'We-ness' to control, manipulate, and harm through collective identity. By examining historical and contemporary examples, we'll uncover how "We-ness" can be twisted into a tool for oppression and violence. We'll also discuss the warning signs of toxic "We-ness" and how to protect against its harmful effects.

The Mafia: Loyalty to the Group Above All Else

Criminal organizations like the Mafia are another example of how "We-ness" can be used to enforce loyalty and protect bad actors. The Mafia, or any criminal gang, operates on a strong sense of group identity and loyalty, often referred to as *omertà*—a code of silence and honour that forbids members from cooperating with authorities or betraying the group.

Rituals, symbols, and a shared understanding of the group's values and norms reinforce this sense of 'We-ness' within the Mafia. New members, or solidarity, undergo initiation ceremonies that symbolize their entry into a brotherhood, where loyalty to the group supersedes all other obligations, including those to family and law. Once inducted, the expectation from the members is to put the group's interests above all else, even if it means engaging in illegal activities or committing violence. The collective identity within the Mafia is so powerful that it not only facilitates criminal activities but also protects those who engage in them. Members who betray the group, known as *pentiti* (turncoats), are often subject to severe punishment, including death.

This intense in-group loyalty and the fear of retribution make it difficult for law enforcement to infiltrate and dismantle these organizations. The Mafia manipulates 'We-ness' to enforce loyalty and silence, creating a culture of fear and obedience through collective identity. It shows how the bonds of group identity, when tied to criminality and violence, can perpetuate harm and protect those who commit it.

The Bernie Madoff Story: A Tale of Trust, Betrayal, and Exploited "We-ness"

The New York finance circle once viewed Bernie Madoff as a legend. He built his reputation as a savvy investor, innovated to shape Wall Street, and earned respect within the Jewish community.

But behind the curtain of his success, Madoff orchestrated one of the largest Ponzi schemes in history. This scheme would ultimately devastate thousands of investors, many of them part of his close-knit Jewish circles. Madoff's ability to exploit the sense of "We-ness" within his community allowed him to perpetuate this fraud for decades. It is how it all began, thrived, and tragically ended.

The Rise of Bernie Madoff: A Man of Prestige and Trust

Bernie Madoff's journey started humbly. Born in 1938 in Queens, New York, to a Jewish family, Madoff wasn't born into wealth but had ambition. In 1960, he founded Bernard L. Madoff Investment Securities, a small trading firm, with a few thousand dollars earned from working as a lifeguard and sprinkler installer.

Over the years, Madoff's firm grew steadily, and his reputation on Wall Street blossomed. He pioneered computer technology in stock trading and developed NASDAQ, becoming its first chairman. This innovative edge cemented his status as a financial visionary. As Madoff's influence grew in the financial world, so did his standing within the Jewish community. He became known as a philanthropist, generously donating to Jewish causes, charities, and institutions.

His wealth, connections, and generosity made him respected in Jewish social and business circles. He served on boards of influential organizations like Yeshiva University and cultivated an image of a trustworthy, successful man who shared the values of the community he supported.

This sense of shared identity—the "We-ness" Madoff cultivated—was central to his ability to build trust. People saw him not just as a financial advisor but as one of them—a pillar of the Jewish community they trusted to manage the wealth of individuals, families, and organizations sharing his background, culture, and values.

The Ponzi Scheme Begins: Trust as a Tool for Deception

Behind the scenes, Madoff wasn't the financial genius he appeared to be. He had been running a Ponzi scheme since at least the early 1990s, though some believe it may have started earlier. The mechanics of a Ponzi scheme are simple: Madoff promised high and consistent returns to investors, but instead of generating those returns through legitimate investments, he used the money from new investors to pay off earlier ones. As long as more money kept flowing in, the scheme remained intact.

But why did so many people, including sophisticated investors, fall for Madoff's scheme? The answer lies in Madoff's ability to tap into the deep trust within the Jewish community. Madoff primarily targeted affluent Jewish individuals, families, and charitable organizations. His connection to Jewish causes and his presence in Jewish philanthropic circles gave him access to an elite network that believed in him implicitly. These weren't just random investors—they were part of his community and felt a strong sense of "We-ness" with Madoff.

One of Madoff's key strategies was creating an aura of exclusivity. He made his investment services appear selective, available only to a privileged few. It reinforces the idea that those "in" were part of an elite, trusted circle. This sense of being in the inner circle further solidified the loyalty and trust of his investors. His returns were steady, even during market downturns, adding to his credibility. Madoff's investors saw him as a financial wizard who was looking out for their interests because, after all, he was one of them.

The Explosion of the Scheme: How "We-ness" Fuelled the Ponzi Machine

Madoff's scheme grew more extensive and complex as the years went on. He attracted individuals and large institutional investors, hedge funds, and even charitable foundations. His operation expanded internationally, but the core of his investor base remained closely tied to the Jewish community. Charitable organizations, including prominent Jewish foundations and institutions, entrusted him with their endowments, convinced that their money was safe with someone who shared their values and commitment to the community.

Among the most high-profile victims was Yeshiva University, where Madoff was a board of trustees member. The university lost over $100 million when the Ponzi scheme collapsed. Madoff's scheme also devastated the Jewish Foundation of Los Angeles and the Elie Wiesel Foundation for Humanity, which lost its entire $15.2 million endowment. These were not just financial losses—these were betrayals of institutions that had been the lifeblood of their communities, committed to charitable causes, education, and cultural preservation.

Madoff's fraud extended beyond the Jewish community, impacting individuals and organizations worldwide. Still, he caused the most profound damage within the tight-knit circles that relied on his credibility. He exploited the bonds of 'We-ness' designed to protect and strengthen communities to deceive and defraud them.

The Collapse: Betrayal and the End of the Illusion

In December 2008, as the global financial crisis deepened, the cracks in Madoff's scheme began to show. With markets collapsing, more investors started requesting withdrawals. Madoff, unable to meet the growing demands, knew the scheme was unravelling.

On December 11, 2008, he got arrested by the FBI after confessing to his sons that his investment firm was "one big lie." The news of his arrest sent shockwaves through the financial world, and the accurate scale of his Ponzi scheme—a staggering $65 billion—was revealed. The fallout from Madoff's collapse was catastrophic financially and emotionally. His investors, who considered him a trusted friend, felt personally betrayed.

The Jewish community, in particular, was left grappling with the devastating impact of his actions. Madoff hadn't just stolen money—he had stolen trust. His deception cut deeply, shattering the bonds of unity and shared identity that had allowed him to rise so high in the first place.

The Aftermath: Lessons from the Exploitation of "We-ness"

Bernie Madoff was sentenced to 150 years in prison for his crimes, but could never undo the damage he caused to individuals, families, and institutions. Many of his victims were left bankrupt, and several charitable organizations had to close their doors forever.

The Madoff Ponzi scheme is a powerful reminder of how the principle of "We-ness"—the sense of belonging and shared identity that brings people together—is exploited for unethical purposes. Madoff used his status within the Jewish community, philanthropic reputation, and personal connections to build an empire of deceit. By making people feel that they were part of an exclusive, trusted circle, he could operate his scheme for decades without raising suspicion.

This story highlights the dangers of blind trust, even within tight-knit communities. While unity and a shared sense of identity can foster solid and supportive relationships, they can also make people more vulnerable to manipulation. Madoff exploited the very bonds of trust that should have protected his victims, turning a source of strength into a tool of deception.

Ultimately, the Bernie Madoff scandal is not just a story of financial fraud—it's a story of how one man exploited "We-ness" to destroy the trust and unity of an entire community.

Labour Unions: The Double-Edged Sword of Solidarity

Labour unions have historically been a force for good, fighting for workers' rights, fair wages, and safe working conditions. They exemplify the positive aspects of "We-ness," where collective identity and solidarity empower individuals to stand up against exploitation. However, even in the context of labour unions, "We-ness" can sometimes take on a darker tone, leading to protectionism, exclusion, and even corruption.

In some cases, labour unions have used their collective power to protect workers and shield bad actors from accountability. For instance, unions may resist efforts to discipline or dismiss members who engage in misconduct, arguing that such actions threaten the unity and strength of the group. It leads to a culture of impunity, where members feel protected by the group regardless of their behaviour.

I have a friend who owns a factory, and he told me about this very thing and how it affected his father's business. In Bangalore, Peenya houses many small-scale industries. These are SMEs or MSMEs that employ factory workers. In my friend's factory, a worker got caught stealing and asked to resign.

Since this worker is a member of a labour group representing this area, he approached the group. Instead of finding what was wrong, the group got in their "We-ness" and protected the worker and made their group relevant, protested against the factory, and vandalized, causing crores of loss.

Another example of this occurs in the case of some police unions across many countries. Critics often accuse police unions of defending officers involved in questionable or illegal actions during high-profile incidents of police misconduct, making it difficult to hold them accountable.

This protective stance, rooted in a strong sense of "We-ness" among union members, fails to realize their actions ultimately erode public trust and perpetuate systemic issues within the organization.

As with any group, the challenge with labour unions is balancing the need for solidarity and collective action with accountability and ethical behaviour. When "We-ness" becomes too insular or protective, it can lead to adverse outcomes that undermine the values the group was formed to uphold.

Cult Groups: The Power of Manipulative "We-ness"

Cults are perhaps the most extreme example of how "We-ness" can be exploited to manipulate and control individuals. Cult leaders often create a strong collective identity that binds members together in an insular, highly controlled environment. This sense of "We-ness" is cultivated through common enemies, shared beliefs, rituals, and language that reinforce the group's ideology and isolate members from outside influences.

One of the most notorious examples is the People's Temple, led by Jim Jones in the USA. What began as a religious movement advocating for social justice and equality turned into a dangerous cult that ended in tragedy.

Jones used the power of "We-ness" to create unquestioning loyalty and obedience among his followers. He presented himself as the sole source of truth and salvation, convincing his followers that they were part of a unique, chosen group. This strong sense of collective identity made members isolate themselves from family and friends who were not part of the group, deepening their dependence on Jones.

The ultimate demonstration of the dark side of "We-ness" in the People's Temple came in 1978 when Jones led over 900 of his followers to commit mass suicide in Jonestown, Guyana. Cult leaders carefully craft the collective identity and use it to justify and enforce horrifying acts of violence against the members themselves and their children.

The Jonestown massacre is a stark reminder of how "We-ness" can be weaponized by charismatic leaders to manipulate and control others to the point of self-destruction.

Religious Extremism: The Perils of Absolute "We-ness"

Religious groups can also be fertile ground for the harmful effects of "We-ness," mainly when leaders use religious ideology to foster an extreme sense of in-group loyalty and out-group hostility. When religion starts promoting a common external enemy and instilling beliefs around that, then it can become a justification for violence and oppression.

Throughout history, we have many examples of this, but recently, the rise of religious extremist groups such as ISIS (Islamic State of Iraq and Syria) is the perfect case. ISIS exploited the concept of "We-ness" to create a powerful, unifying identity among its followers, but also portrayed the common enemy as anyone outside Islam. Through a mix of religious rhetoric, propaganda, and social media outreach, ISIS framed its cause as a holy war, positioning its members as part of a righteous struggle against a corrupt and evil world. This sense of "We-ness" was used to recruit individuals from around the globe, many of whom were disillusioned or marginalized in their societies. Once individuals joined ISIS, they were subjected to intense indoctrination, further strengthening their identification with the group.

This process often involved isolating recruits from their previous lives, both physically and psychologically, and instilling a deep hatred of perceived enemies. The collective identity fostered by ISIS was so strong that it led members to commit acts of extreme violence, including suicide bombings and mass executions, in the name of the group.

The case of ISIS demonstrates how "We-ness" can be exploited by extremist leaders to create a rigid, absolutist identity that justifies and perpetuates violence. It highlights the dangers of allowing collective identity to become so all-encompassing that it overrides individual morality and critical thinking.

The Warning Signs of Toxic "We-ness"

Understanding the dark side of "We-ness" is essential for recognizing when collective identity is being manipulated or taken to harmful extremes. Here are some warning signs that "We-ness" is becoming toxic:

1. **Isolation from Outside Influences:** Groups that encourage or enforce isolation from non-members, whether through physical separation or by discouraging contact with outsiders, may be fostering a toxic form of "We-ness." This isolation can make members more susceptible to manipulation and less able to evaluate the group's actions critically.

2. **Demonization of Outsiders:** When a group frames outsiders as enemies or threats, it creates a dangerous "us versus them" mentality. It leads to dehumanization, where members view those outside the group as less deserving of empathy or respect, justifying harmful actions against them.

3. **Unquestioning Loyalty and Obedience:** Groups that demand absolute loyalty and discourage questioning or dissent are at risk of developing toxic

"We-ness." In such environments, members may feel pressured to conform to the group's norms, even when they conflict with their personal values or ethical standards.

4. **Protection of Wrongdoers:** When a group prioritizes loyalty over accountability, protecting members who engage in misconduct creates a culture of impunity. It can perpetuate harmful behaviours and undermine the group's integrity.

5. **Exclusivity and Elitism:** Groups that foster a sense of superiority or elitism, where members believe they are better than or fundamentally different from outsiders, may be cultivating a toxic "We-ness." It leads to divisiveness and conflict within the group and with others.

Mitigating the Harmful Effects of "We-ness"

While the dark side of "We-ness" is a serious concern, it's important to remember again that collective identity itself isn't inherently wrong. The key is to foster healthy "We-ness" that promotes inclusion, accountability, and ethical behaviour. Here are some strategies for mitigating the harmful effects of "We-ness":

1. **Encourage Critical Thinking:** Promote a culture of valuing questioning and critical thinking, encouraging

students and employees to reflect on the group's actions and beliefs and speak up when something doesn't align with values. It helps to prevent groupthink and the uncritical acceptance of harmful norms.

2. **Foster Inclusive "We-ness":** Build an inclusive collective identity that welcomes diverse perspectives and experiences. It reduces the likelihood of exclusionary or elitist attitudes and helps create a more resilient, adaptable group.

3. **Promote Transparency and Accountability:** Ensure that the group's leadership is held accountable for its actions and that mechanisms are in place for addressing misconduct. Transparency in decision-making helps to build trust and prevent the abuse of power.

4. **Balance Solidarity with Ethics:** While solidarity is essential, it shouldn't come at the expense of ethical behaviour or group favouritism. Encourage a balance between supporting members and holding them accountable for their actions. It helps to maintain the group's integrity and public trust.

5. **Maintain Open Communication Channels:** Prevent isolation by maintaining open communication channels with those outside the group. It helps counteract echo chambers and ensures the group remains connected to broader societal values and norms.

Chapter 13:

"We-ness":

Building Unity Across Ethnic and Cultural Boundaries

The best way to find out if you can trust somebody is to trust them."

Ernest Hemingway

Throughout history, people have moved across borders countries—whether for work, education, or a better life — and this number is only increasing in today's globalized world.

As these ethnic communities settle in new places, they bring rich cultural traditions, languages, and identities. The challenge and opportunity lie in how these communities maintain their sense of "We-ness" while integrating into their new environments.

Balancing old and new identities often leads to powerful forms of cross-cultural unity that benefit both the communities and the broader society. In this chapter, let us explore how ethnic communities create and sustain "We-ness." Let's also look at how businesses that successfully tap into this cross-cultural "We-ness" achieve remarkable success, leveraging the strength of diverse communities to build inclusive and thriving enterprises.

The Roots of Cross-Cultural "We-ness"

When people move to a new place, like a new country, they often seek out others who share their cultural background to maintain a connection to their roots. It is a natural and profoundly human response to the challenges of migration. The familiar language, customs, and traditions of one's ethnic community provide comfort and continuity, helping individuals navigate the uncertainties of a new environment.

However, forming cross-cultural "We-ness" is still complex and multifaceted. On the one hand, these communities who have migrated to a new country with different languages, food habits, religions, and identities must strive to maintain their distinct cultural identity, passing down traditions, languages, and values to the next generation.

On the other hand, they must also navigate the challenges of integrating into the broader society, which often requires adopting new cultural norms, languages, and social practices.

The result is a dynamic and evolving sense of "We-ness" that bridges the old and the new. People instinctively form ethnic enclaves, as seen in cities worldwide, where neighbourhoods often reflect the cultural diversity of their inhabitants.

When it comes to business, where decision-making ultimately depends on trust, it seems far more accessible to trust one's community vs. others. Whether for lending loans, buying and selling, or even supporting people to settle in new countries, it demands enormous trust.

The "We-ness" drastically eliminates the risks, forming trust when one is part of the same community and due to a sense of belonging.

The Economic Power of Ethnic Communities

Ethnic communities that successfully maintain their sense of "We-ness" often create vibrant economic ecosystems that benefit their members and the broader economy. This financial power is particularly evident in the success of immigrant-owned businesses, which usually serve as both cultural hubs and economic engines for their communities.

One striking example is in the United States; the Patel community, mainly belonging to Gujarat of India, is a solid ethnic community. They maintain a strong sense of "We-ness." Because of this, they provide a network of social support, economic opportunities, and cultural preservation for any new person settling in the US or even wanting to establish a career or build a business. This sense of "We-ness" has helped them own the largest motel chains in the US.

Another example I came across from one of my Korean colleagues during my stay in the US was the strong Korean-American business community in Los Angeles. In the aftermath of the 1992 Los Angeles riots, destroying many Korean-owned businesses and the community faced significant challenges. However, the strong sense of "We-ness" within the Korean-American community played a critical role in the recovery and rebuilding process.

Community members pooled resources supported each other's businesses and leveraged their collective identity to rebuild more robustly than before. Today, Korean-Americans are a vital part of Los Angeles' economy, with thriving businesses that range from restaurants and grocery stores to high-tech firms and real estate ventures. The success of these businesses is not just a testament to the resilience of the Korean-American community; it also highlights the economic benefits of cross-cultural "We-ness." Korean-Americans have created enterprises catering to their community and the broader population by maintaining strong ties to their cultural identity.

It has allowed them to preserve their cultural heritage while contributing to the city's economic diversity and vitality. In India, we can see the example in the Marwari business community. For ages, Marwari communities have established themselves as significant economic players. Despite being a minority, the Marwari community has maintained a strong sense of "We-ness" through cultural practices, language, and business networks. These networks have enabled them to thrive economically, often dominating key sectors such as finance, retail, trading, and manufacturing.

The economic success of these communities is not just about financial gains; it's also about the role that "We-ness" plays in fostering trust, cooperation, and mutual support. Trust is often built on shared cultural values and social norms within these business networks, leading to more effective collaboration and better business outcomes. This sense of collective identity provides a competitive advantage, allowing these communities to navigate challenges and seize opportunities in ways that might be more difficult for others.

Balancing Identity and Integration

For ethnic communities, one of the critical challenges of cross-cultural "We-ness" is balancing preserving their cultural identity with the need to integrate into the broader society. This balance is crucial for maintaining social cohesion and ensuring the community thrives in its new environment.

One approach that has proven successful is the concept of "integration without assimilation." This approach allows ethnic communities to retain their cultural identity while also becoming active participants in the broader society. It involves adopting elements of the new culture—

language, education, and civic engagement—while continuing to celebrate and preserve one's cultural heritage.

A prime example of this is the Jewish diaspora in the United States. Jewish communities have maintained a strong sense of "We-ness" through religious practices, cultural traditions, and communal institutions like synagogues and Jewish schools. At the same time, American Jews have been deeply integrated into the broader society, making significant contributions to fields such as law, science, the arts, and business. This dual identity has allowed Jewish Americans to thrive as a distinct community and part of the broader fabric of American life.

The Role of Businesses in Fostering Cross-Cultural "We-ness"

Understanding the power of "We-ness" and Unity to influence, many businesses find unique opportunities to foster cross-cultural "We-ness" by creating environments that celebrate diversity and promote inclusion. At the outset, this seems to benefit the company by attracting a diverse workforce and customer base, but it is not easier to create social cohesion by bringing people who hold strong beliefs or identities together.

One example is multinational corporations like Google and Microsoft, which have made diversity and inclusion central to their corporate culture.

These companies recognize that a diverse workforce brings a wide range of perspectives, ideas, and experiences, which can lead to more incredible innovation and better business outcomes.

By creating a sense of "We-ness" that transcends cultural and ethnic boundaries, these companies aim to build strong, cohesive teams capable of tackling complex global challenges. But so far, there has been a lot of criticism about this. In the name of DEI, companies are forcefully not hiring based on merit, affecting overall business performance. Another example is Unilever, which has successfully integrated diversity and inclusion into its global strategy, reflecting Unilever's commitment to inclusivity in its marketing campaigns, product development, and corporate practices.

For instance, the company's Dove "Real Beauty" campaign challenges traditional beauty standards by featuring women of different ages, sizes, and ethnicities. This campaign resonated with a diverse audience and reinforced the idea that beauty comes in many forms, fostering a sense of "We-ness" that is inclusive and empowering. Businesses can also support ethnic communities by providing resources, mentorship, and growth opportunities. For example, companies that partner with local ethnic chambers of commerce or community organizations to support their businesses. It helps these businesses thrive and strengthens the broader economy by promoting entrepreneurship and job creation within ethnic communities.

Embracing Cross-Cultural "We-ness" for a Better Future

Cross-cultural "We-ness" is a dynamic and evolving process that reflects the complexities of our globalized world. For ethnic communities, it offers a way to maintain a connection to their cultural heritage while integrating into their new environment. For businesses, it provides a pathway to success by tapping into the strength of diversity and inclusion. By embracing cross-cultural "We-ness," we can build stronger, more resilient communities that celebrate the richness of our differences while finding common ground in our shared humanity.

We can create a world where unity and diversity coexist, enriching our lives and societies.

Chapter 14:

Leveraging Diversity in "We-ness": Hindu Way of Living

This Motherland (earth in general and India or Bharat in specific) shelters and nourishes (without any discrimination) people who speak different languages, follow various customs, and have different thought processes, like people living in the same house (members of a family).

Atharva Veda Prithvi Suktam 12.1.45

I was unsure about adding this chapter as this topic can take a book by itself, and there indeed exist more experts on this matter. But then, as I researched, I found not many have attempted to answer Hindu Unity using the human psychology, evolution, and philosophy aspects together.

So here is a small attempt to raise the curiosity and awareness of readers so they can explore this topic further.

The Paradox of Unity in Diversity

So far, we have discussed the strength of unity and collective identity, how it is rooted in the human psyche, the need for belonging, and the evolution of tribal nature. But unity in itself is a tribal nature. There is either win-lose option. The "We" vs. "They" harbours competition and wins at any cost, and winning is the ultimate "value". It is useful in businesses, sports, and other areas with enough laws to ensure that groups do not cross ethical boundaries and operate within the prescribed rules.

However, when tribal nature extends to areas such as politics, between nations, and religion, it creates more harm than good. Because here, what is required is a means of co-existence vs win-lose propositions. Throughout history, among empires and today, contemporary politics and religions have shown that tribal natures extend to these areas, and it leads to extreme violence and hatred.

But can humans overcome our tribal nature in every area of life and coexist as a giant "We-Group"?

Yes, indeed, it is possible, and I would like to offer that perspective of how diversity in "We-ness" and the Hindu way of life fosters diversity and creates unity. At first glance, the idea of unity with diversity might seem paradoxical. How can a group be united when its members are so different? The answer lies in understanding that unity doesn't require uniformity.

We can build a solid collective identity on the differences that distinguish us from one another. When diverse individuals come together, bringing their unique perspectives, experiences, and talents, the group becomes more prosperous, innovative, and resilient. The metaphor of a mosaic beautifully illustrates this concept, showing how each piece, with its distinct colour and shape, contributes to the overall beauty and coherence of the design. In a mosaic, it's not the sameness of the pieces that create the image; it's their diversity.

We see this everywhere in nature. Whether it is forests, ocean bottom, or wild animals, so much diversity binds everything together. Similarly, each group's different contributions create a vibrant, dynamic culture in a diverse society. Among all the nations, India is perhaps the most striking example of unity with diversity. The country is home to over 1.4 billion people, speaking over 19,500 languages and dialects, practising multiple religions, and living in various cultural contexts. Yet, despite—or perhaps because of—this diversity, there is a strong sense of Indian identity that binds these diverse communities together. This sense of "We-ness" is not about erasing differences but celebrating them as part of a larger, unified whole.

The Role of Hindu Culture in Fostering Unity in Diversity

Sanatana Dharma, which means Sanatana as Eternal and Dharma—Righteous living, has shaped Indian society for thousands of years. It provides a robust framework for understanding how diversity can lead to unity. It comes from one of the core principles of Hindu philosophy, which is the idea of *Vasudhaiva Kutumbakam*.

ayaṁ nijaḥ paro veti gaṇanā laghu-cetasām |
udāra-caritānāṁ tu vasudhaiva kuṭumbakam ||
(Hitopadeśa: Mitra-lābhaḥ, 71)

When one sees another human being, the feeling comes to the small-minded, "Is this person one among 'us' or of 'others'?" Whereas those of magnanimous character, have the broad feeling that the entire earth is their family.

Vasudhaiva Kutumbakam. means "the world is one family." This value and principle emphasize the interconnectedness of all beings, regardless of their differences.

It teaches that diversity is not a barrier to unity and is a natural expression of the underlying oneness of existence. Hinduism is a diverse tradition, encompassing many faiths, symbols, rituals, languages, and even philosophies.

When we look into the unity framework and the nine elements that make up unity, we can see in Sanatana Dharma that there is no founder or leader, no central religious authority, no uniform set of doctrines or beliefs, and no common enemy.

To compensate for this, there is significant emphasis on who we are, collective values or principles, shared language, shared rituals, symbols, and stories. So, any group that lacks a central leader, common enemy, and beliefs is more egalitarian. It allows individuals to practice faith according to their personality and duties, not group norms. It is critical because enforcing strong norms makes practising spirituality more dogmatic.

At the core philosophy of Hindu Dharma exists the premise that identifying self and collective identity is helpful for existence or a survival mechanism, but these shouldn't limit the individual from experiencing universal identity. Hence, the few core values of Hindu Dharma are,

1. **Lokah Samastah Sukinho Bhavantu**: May All Beings Everywhere Be Happy and Free

2. **Vasudhaiva Kutumbakam**: The world is one big family

3. **Ahimso paramo dharma:** Non-violence is the righteous duty

4. **ekam sat vipra bahudha vadanti:** There is one truth: sages say different ways

5. janani janmabhoomischa swargadapi gariyasi: Nation & Mother is holier than heaven

6. **Sathyameva Jayathe**–Truth (Existence) Always Wins

This level of universal inclusivity has allowed Hinduism to accommodate a vast diversity of practices and faiths, from the monistic practices of Buddhist Jain monks to the devotion of Shaivism, Vaishnavism worshippers, from the philosophical inquiries of Vedanta to the rituals of village deities.

Also, only in India did many new faiths originate, and they have survived and thrived.

This pluralistic approach has helped foster a tolerance and acceptance culture in India. Instead of seeking to impose a single way of life on all, Hindu culture encourages people to respect and learn from each other's differences. It has created a society where diverse communities—whether defined by religion, language, or ethnicity—can coexist peacefully while maintaining their distinct identities.

A prime example of this is the celebration of festivals in India. Different communities celebrate festivals with unique customs and rituals throughout the year. Yet, these celebrations are not isolated events; they are often shared across communities, with people of different backgrounds participating in each other's festivals.

How Unity with Diversity Can Thrive

Starting from the 10th century, India was invaded by Islamic rulers. In contrast to Hinduism, Islam is a more unified religion, emphasizing monotheism, and the Quran's centrality. While there are different sects within Islam, Muslims around the world bond over common brotherhood.

When it comes to the elements of Unity, Muslims have a clear set of shared beliefs and practices, identify with the leader and also want to identify with the common enemy

(Kafir), which means those who do not practice Islam. This unity in Islam has historically given it a strong sense of identity and purpose, especially in the context of religious and cultural interactions. It has enabled Muslim communities to organize effectively, spread their faith, and assert their influence in various parts of the world.

Also, the Unity of Muslims is more rooted in evolutionary ways and seeks to win over co-existence. That is why some extreme sections of Muslim groups consider common enemies as those who are non-Muslims. When confronted with external invaders who believe that non-Muslims are enemies and co-existence with others who do not practice the Muslim religion is blasphemy, then it is bound to create violence.

Time and again, it has shown that to face united forces who bring in extreme elements of the tribal nature, the diverse communities must unite by bringing the elements of unity, such as strong leadership, a common enemy, slogans, and stories. The perfect example again is Shivaji during the 17th century, the founder of the Maratha Kingdom, who united Hindus against the Mughals. Mughals had already ruled India for almost 150 years and controlled 3/4th of India at that time.

It was when the Hindu faith was tested and even faced extinction.

Shivaji offered resistance by being the leader of Hindus and also making Mughals a Hindu's core enemy. He developed slogans like Hindavi Swarajya to mean "Hindu independence from foreign rule". In doing this, it created a sense of unity among factions of many Hindu communities and history reveals Maratha became victorious over the Mughals and ruled 80% of India for the next 100 years before the British gained strength.

Similarly, during Indian independence, leaders like Netaji and Savarkar were able to unite people for a specific cause of the fight against the British and later sustain the unity of Hindus. Time and again, leadership and identification of external common enemies become consistent needs to unify diverse communities. In contemporary politics also, it is widespread for political parties to create vote banks by uniting sections of society in the name of race, religion, and caste.

These vote banks seem united and do exhibit strong "we-ness" but are not long-lasting as they serve a narrow set of values and vision! They create a further tribal nature that does not serve the larger purpose of uniting the nation.

Finally, overcoming the tribal nature of winning over others at the cost of even violence, is possible only by recognizing our uniqueness and embracing the idea that we are all part of a larger community, adopting the values of *Vasudhaiva Kutumbakam*—the world as one family.

This offers a powerful reminder of the importance of "We-group" with diversity, and overcoming divisions that the world needs to learn and imbibe.

This principle has universal applicability in an increasingly interconnected and interdependent world.

Chapter 15:

The Future of "We-ness" in an Ever-Changing World

"Alone, we can do so little; together, we can do so much."

Helen Keller

As we move further into the more and more connected world with AI and social platforms, nuclear families, the concept of "We-ness" is evolving in ways we could never have imagined just a few decades ago. The rapid pace of technological advancement, the increasing interconnectedness of global communities, and the shifting dynamics of power and influence are all reshaping how we form, maintain, and understand collective identity.

In this final chapter, let's explore the future of "We-ness," focusing on the challenges and opportunities ahead. We'll delve into how emerging trends will probably impact our sense of unity and belonging and what this means for communities, businesses, and societies.

The Globalization of "We-ness"

Globalization over the last few decades has already blurred the lines between local and global identities. As people, ideas, and cultures move more freely across borders, the concept of "We-ness" is becoming more complex and multi-layered. For many, this means navigating multiple identities—being part of a local community and identifying as a global citizen.

This globalization of "We-ness" presents both opportunities and challenges. On the one hand, it allows us to build connections across cultures and create a more inclusive, interconnected world. The boundaries of our birthplace or nationality no longer limit us; we now choose to join global movements, causes, and communities that align with our values and passions.

However, this new global "We" can also lead to tensions and conflicts as different identities and loyalties come into play. For example, as people migrate for better opportunities, they often bring their cultural identities with them, which can sometimes clash with the dominant culture of their new home. It can create friction and division, particularly if communities feel that their sense of "We-ness" is being threatened by outsiders.

The key to navigating this complex landscape is to embrace a more inclusive and flexible understanding of "We-ness." It means recognizing that identity is not a zero-sum game—belonging to one group doesn't mean you can't also belong to another. It's possible to be rooted in a local community and connected to a global network to celebrate your cultural heritage while embracing new experiences and perspectives.

For example, my home city, Bangalore, over the last 2 decades, has experienced a tremendous inflow of people from all over India, as Bangalore's economy boomed due to the software industry. The people who have made their home in Bangalore, say Bengali, Punjabi, Tamil, or Marathi, can always be a part of their community in Bangalore and harness their strength of unity. At the same time, learning Kannada's local language and being part of any local culture builds more inclusivity. Otherwise, there will be multiple We-groups that do have conflicts!

Similarly, as businesses and organizations operate in an increasingly globalized world, they too must adapt to this more nuanced understanding of "We-ness." It requires creating environments that respect and celebrate diversity while fostering a shared sense of purpose and belonging. Companies that succeed in this will be those that can balance the local and the global, the individual and the collective, in ways that resonate with employees and customers.

Take a company like Amazon, Uber, or Zomato. These companies come with colossal capital, technology access, and a willingness to disrupt the existing way of doing business. When Uber entered India, there were many taxi & Auto unions. These taxi unions, though united, also never acted in customers' best interest. As discussed earlier, the dark side of unity gets taken over, and bad actors never get punished.

When Uber started operations, it was a welcome change for the commuters, who embraced it. Now, there are reports of Uber monopolizing commutes! Similar to Amazon or other global businesses that dominate local cultures and traditions can sometimes be overshadowed or diluted. The rise of international institutions—whether in finance, politics, or technology—further complicates this landscape, often leading to the standardization of practices, values, and lifestyles. For smaller communities, the challenge is to retain their sense of "We-ness" in a world that often prioritizes uniformity over diversity. It is challenging when young people, usually more connected to global trends through the internet and social media, begin to adopt values and practices that differ from those of their elders. The fear of losing cultural heritage, language, and traditional ways of life is a genuine concern for many communities. Similarly, smaller nationalities face the challenge of asserting their identity within more significant political and economic unions.

Balancing the Local and the Global

One of the critical challenges for both smaller communities and global businesses is finding the right balance between the local and the global. For communities, this means preserving their unique identity and traditions while engaging with the broader world. For businesses, it means maintaining a consistent global brand while adapting to local markets and respecting cultural differences.

The key to achieving this balance lies in the concept of "glocalization"—a term that combines "globalization" and "localization." Glocalization involves adapting global strategies to fit local contexts, ensuring they resonate with local values, needs, and preferences. This approach allows smaller communities to assert their identity on the global stage while benefiting from globalization opportunities. Similarly, it will enable businesses to build a strong international brand that feels relevant and authentic in different markets.

The Evolution of "We-ness" in Business

The evolution of "We-ness" will be closely tied to how businesses adapt to changing consumer expectations and workplace dynamics. In an era where purpose-driven brands are increasingly valued, companies go beyond traditional marketing and create genuine connections with their customers.

It means building communities around shared values, fostering customer loyalty through authentic engagement, and creating products and services that resonate more deeply. Co-creation is one of the powerful concepts that promotes unity. Unity is between internal teams, clients, or institutions. Co-creation has revealed that people are more willing to help each other, and there is more collaboration and cooperativeness, resulting in boosted performance. Another way businesses can achieve this is by embracing transparency and authenticity in their communications. Customers today are more informed and discerning than ever, and they expect brands to be honest and accountable. Companies that are open about their practices listen to their customers and respond to customers' concerns. They are well positioned to build lasting relationships and a strong sense of "We-ness."

Moreover, businesses that are proactive in fostering collaboration and knowledge sharing across different teams, departments, and regions. In a world where remote work and digital collaboration are going only to grow, creating a sense of unity with a dispersed workforce is crucial. It requires investing in the right tools and platforms and creating rituals and practices that unite people, even when they're physically apart.

Finally, every business must prepare to evolve with their customers and employees. The concept of "We-ness" is not static; it will continue to change as new technologies, trends, and challenges emerge. Companies willing to adapt, listen, and learn will be better equipped to create and sustain unity in an ever-changing world.

For example, companies such as Starbucks have successfully applied the principles of glocalization by adapting their stores and products to reflect local cultures while maintaining their core brand identity. Starbucks has incorporated traditional Chinese elements into its store design in China and offers products that cater to local tastes, such as green tea lattes and mooncakes.

At the same time, the company maintains its global brand identity, creating a sense of "We-ness" among customers and employees that spans both local and global contexts.

Another notable development is the launch of ONDC (Open Network for Digital Commerce) by the Indian government. Through this ONDC, the Indian government wants to provide a level playing field to connect millions of small retailers, distributors, producers, or manufacturers to consumers on the typical digital commerce platform.

This creates an alternative platform for Amazon, Uber, and Zomato. ONDC's mission is to offer the best in technology to each of the players in the business and create a sense of community to support everyone in the e-commerce chain.

Conclusion: Unity in a Connected World

The forces of globalization and institutionalization present both challenges and opportunities for sustaining "We-ness." Whether in smaller communities or global businesses, the key is to find a balance between the local and the global, the unique and the universal.

By embracing diversity, fostering inclusivity, and leveraging the power of symbols, rituals, and shared values, we can create a sense of unity that is resilient and also adaptable. As we conclude this exploration of "We-ness," it's clear that the concept of collective identity is more relevant than ever in our interconnected world.

Whether we are building communities, leading organizations, or navigating cultural change, the principles of "We-ness" provide a powerful framework for creating unity, bringing collaboration, and driving positive change.

Together, we can build a world where diversity and unity go hand in hand, enriching our lives and strengthening our collective future.

Epilogue

The Power of Unity in Action

As I bring this book to a close, I want to share two stories that illustrate the transformative power of "We-ness" not in any business, or politics, but in our everyday individual lives. These are not just stories of individual success—they're stories of how unity and community can help us achieve what once felt out of reach.

Story 1: Fitness Through Community

Cult. Fit is a new-age gym that has revitalized the fitness culture in India using the concept of "we-ness". The slogan of "We are Cult" creates a sense of community that is hard to find in standalone gyms. I experienced this first-hand as I joined Cult. Fit a few months back. Though I have been to many gyms and fitness centres, I could see immediately the "we-group" effect Cult. Fit has been created.

Here I met a Vijay whose story continues to inspire me. He had just completed his 3,600th workout class—a streak that spanned over 5 years. It wasn't just the number of classes that amazed me; it was his journey to get there.

I became curious as I got to know this and asked him, what made this difference. Vijay said, that before joining Cult, he struggled with consistency in his fitness routine. He would join gyms, work out for a while, and eventually quit. Motivation would wane, and life would take over. But everything changed after he joined Cult Fitness.

What made the difference? Community. Cult.fit doesn't just provide a space to exercise; it gives him a sense of belonging. The group classes, the other members he found who are on the same journey, the slogan of "We are cult" at the end of every session, articulating values, and sharing of stories of other members all created a sense of belonging. This is what created an environment where he felt motivated and accountable. His individual struggle transformed into a collective mission, and the We-ness of the group helped him develop a habit he could sustain.

Story 2: Writing My First Book

The second story is my own. For years, I had dreamed of publishing a book. I started and stopped, scribbled ideas, and even wrote a few drafts, but I could never sustain the effort. Life got in the way, self-doubt crept in, and the goal of finishing my book always seemed to slip further out of reach.

Then, six months ago, everything changed. I joined a community called Author Freedom Hub (AFH), started by Som Bathla, to help budding authors publish their books. As I joined the group, for the first time, I wasn't alone in my journey. I was surrounded by people who shared the same vision, values, and goals.

The We-ness of the group fuelled my progress. The accountability, encouragement, and shared purpose turned what once felt daunting into something achievable. Not only did I finish my book, but I'm now well on my way to publishing my second.

This experience taught me an invaluable lesson: when we struggle to achieve our goals, the missing ingredient is often not more effort. It's finding the right community—a group of people who share our vision and can influence us to keep moving forward.

The Ripple Effect of Unity

These stories are reminders that we're not meant to achieve our goals alone. Whether it's fitness, writing, or any other challenge, the power of "We-ness" can help us overcome obstacles, change behaviours, and accomplish things we never thought possible.

If you are struggling to hit your goals, the answer may be simpler than you think. Find a community that shares your vision and values.

Surround yourself with people who lift you and hold you accountable. Together, you'll discover that what once felt impossible becomes achievable.

The future isn't about "I"—it's about "We."

Thank you for being part of this journey.

Did You Enjoy This Book?

Congratulations and thank you for completing this book! I hope you'll put what you've read to good use.

If you have a minute, it would mean so much to me if you would review the book online. Your review goes a long way towards encouraging other people to read The Power Of We and I would consider it a huge personal favour.

Thank you in advance! Please go to:

www.prashgodrehal.com/ReviewPowerOfWe

Additionally, Please send any questions, comments, edits or feedback to: www.prashgodrehal.com/Contact

Sincerest Thanks

Prashanth

Summary - Chapter Takeaways

PART 1: WHAT MAKES UNITY POWERFUL FOR INFLUENCE

- **Chapter 1:** Unity is the invisible glue that binds people, movements, and communities, driving collective action and influencing behaviour beyond individual efforts.

- **Chapter 2:** "We-ness" is rooted in our psychological need to belong and is the foundation of trust, loyalty, and shared identity in any group.

- **Chapter 3:** Unity comes from the tribal nature and it is evolutionary. The evolutionary means to protect and serve one's group is far stronger than many other influence means.

PART 2: THE BLUEPRINT OF FORMING WE-GROUP

- **Chapter 4:** 9 essential elements go into forming strong groups. The first one is, that defining clear boundaries for who belongs and who doesn't create focus and strengthen group identity, but it must be done thoughtfully to avoid exclusionary harm.

- **Chapter 5:** Shared values and beliefs act as the moral compass of a group, ensuring cohesion and inspiring deep emotional connections.

- **Chapter 6**: A compelling collective vision inspires individuals to work toward a shared future, creating alignment and long-term commitment. Identifying a common enemy can unite groups by focusing energy and purpose, but it must be used ethically to avoid fostering negativity or division.

- **Chapter 7:** Great leaders unify their teams by embodying shared values, fostering belonging, and rallying people around a clear vision and purpose.

- **Chapter 8:** Shared language fosters a sense of belonging and alignment, turning groups into unified communities with a common identity.

- **Chapter 9**: Rituals and symbols create emotional anchors that solidify group identity and keep members connected to shared traditions and goals.

- **Chapter 10**: Stories are the heart of unity, giving life to shared struggles, victories, and values that inspire and bind groups together.

PART 3: OBSERVING WE-NESS EVERYWHERE

- **Chapter 11**: Digital platforms like social media amplify the reach of "We-ness," but as leaders, one must navigate challenges like groupthink, conformity, and the dark side of online influence.

- **Chapter 12:** Unity is powerful but can be misused by bad actors to manipulate, exclude, or exploit, underscoring the need for ethical leadership.

- **Chapter 13**: Worldwide ethnic groups show how unity is key to sustaining their communities and helps them thrive in foreign lands

- **Chapter 14**: Diversity strengthens unity by bringing unique perspectives into a shared mission, proving that unity doesn't mean uniformity. Hindu way of life teaches that common enemy and rigid beliefs are not the answer to co-existence

- **Chapter 15**: In an interconnected world, embracing the principles of unity will be critical to building stronger brands, communities, and movements that thrive in the future.

Acknowledgements

Bringing *The Power of We* to life has been a journey filled with support, encouragement, and inspiration from many incredible people. First, I want to thank Dr. Robert Cialdini, whose concept of Unity, introduced in the latest edition of *Influence: The Psychology of Persuasion*, sparked the idea for this book. His work inspired me to explore the fascinating dynamics of human behaviour and collective identity. I'm grateful to Mr. Krishna G, my business partner and brother, for always encouraging me to take on this project with confidence. I also want to thank the Cialdini community for their support and the Author Freedom Hub (AFH), a group of self-reliant creators who provided invaluable guidance to help me navigate the process of writing and publishing this book.

My family has been my biggest source of strength throughout this journey. To my wife, Renuka, thank you for your unwavering support and understanding. To my daughter, Kshama, for insights into social media gave me new perspectives that shaped parts of this book. And to my young son, Adhokshaj, your energy and joy have been a constant reminder of what truly matters.

Finally, I want to thank family members and friends whose support and encouragement have been essential.

Notes

Books and Articles

1. Cialdini, Robert B. *Influence: The Psychology of Persuasion*. Harper Business, 2006.

2. Godin, Seth. *Tribes: We Need You to Lead Us*. Portfolio, 2008.

3. Social Identity Theory: Henri Tajfel and John Turner devised their *Social Identity Theory*

4. Peer Pressure: Ash Conformity Experiments: socialsci.libretexts.org

5. The common enemy effect under strategic network formation and disruption: Hans Holler, Britta Hoyer https://www.sciencedirect.com/science/article/abs/pii/S0167268119300824

6. Groups & Symbols: On the psychological function of flags and logos: Group identity symbols increase perceived entitativity Shannon P. Callahan. Source: escholorship.org

7. Rituals: The social functions of group rituals, Rachel E. Watson-Jones and Cristine H. Legare. Department of Psychology, The University of Texas at Austin

8. Housel, Morgan. *The Psychology of Money: Timeless Lessons on Wealth, Greed, and Happiness*. Harriman House, 2020

9. Tagore, Rabindranath. *Selected Writings on Literature and Language*. Oxford University Press, 2001

10. Drucker, Peter F. *Managing for Results*. Harper Business, 1993

11. Neuro Coupling: Speaker–listener neural coupling underlies successful communication. Greg J. Stephens, Lauren J. Silbert, and Uri Hasson

Speeches and Interviews 6. Jobs, Steve. "Steve Jobs on Customer Focus," Interview with Steve Jobs (1997). 7. King Jr., Martin Luther. "I Have a Dream." Speech delivered at the Lincoln Memorial, Washington, D.C., August 28, 1963. 8. Mandela, Nelson. *Long Walk to Freedom: The Autobiography of Nelson Mandela*: Little, Brown and Company, 1994.

Online Sources 9. Solis, Brian. "The Art and Science of Listening." Social Media Research Blog, 2011. [URL] 10. Alston, David. Quote on social media influence from digital marketing blogs and resources (specific source reference).

Historical and Religious Texts 11. The Bhagavad Gita is the song of Lord Krishna. 12. Teachings of Buddha, as referenced in *The Dhammapada*. 13. Vivekananda, Swami. *Complete Works of Swami Vivekananda*. Advaita Ashrama, 1957.

Additional Influential Figures Referenced 14. Gandhi, Mahatma. *The Story of My Experiments with Truth*. 15. Buffett, Warren, and Munger, Charlie. *Berkshire Hathaway Annual Letters to Shareholders*. Various years.

Leadership and Influence 16. Nader, Ralph. "The Function of Leadership," speech on civic engagement and leadership. 17. Sinek, Simon. *Start With Why: How Great Leaders Inspire Everyone to Take Action*. Portfolio, 2009.

About the Author

Prashanth Godrehal is Co-Founder of GrowthAspire, a company specialized in helping businesses, professionals achieve their business and career growth aspirations using tools of behavioural insights, neuroscience and ethical persuasion at work.

He is a Cialdini Institute certified coach, and business excellence from Haas School of Business, Berkely, USA Alumni.

Prashanth G has more than 2 decades of experience in leadership, coaching, and entrepreneurship. Passionate about how to turn ideas to reality. Towards Prashanth G leverages his learnings from behavioral insights, neuroscience and persuasive communication to corporate culture, integrating diverse lessons into a singular, actionable guide for leaders across all sectors.

Prashanth G is happily married, with 2 loving children and lives in Bengaluru.

To get in touch with Prashanth G for training programs, coaching, keynote presentations visit www.prashgodrehal.com

www.ingramcontent.com/pod-product-compliance
Lightning Source LLC
Chambersburg PA
CBHW020540160726
47991CB00002B/515